THE PAGAN CHURCH

THE
PAGAN CHURCH

The Protestant Failure in America

RALPH E. DODGE

J. B. Lippincott Company

PHILADELPHIA AND NEW YORK

Foreword

I love my native America, but at the same time I hate her. The contrast of her ugly affluence against the proud poverty of my adopted Africa makes it impossible for me to live happily in either spot, for I always carry the image of the other with me.

It is possible that association with non-Americans has changed my value systems, but each time I return to my homeland I view with shocking freshness what probably has been a growing characteristic of American church life for a long time.

During the course of writing this book, many friends offered help and suggestions while I was mulling over ideas—to them I owe much. I wish especially to thank the following: Miss Betty Thompson, the Reverend Allan R. Brockway, the Reverend Gabriel Setiloane, and Mr. Bengt K. Simonsson, who criticized the manuscript constructively; Ethel T. Elsea, who carefully edited it and rewrote parts; and my wife, Eunice, who contributed mild criticism and constant encouragement.

Ralph E. Dodge
Mindolo Ecumenical Foundation
Kitwe, Zambia
May 17, 1968

Contents

Introduction

Cardinal Souhard once said that France was a land of baptized pagans.[1] Reinhold Niebuhr has observed that the current religious strategy seems to be to bring in the pagan gods and clothe them in Christian garb, hoping that the traditional Christian piety might find its way into the secular forms.[2] What they are both saying is that there are many pagans in the churches, perhaps a few in clerical attire.

Such an individual is technically defined as a "pagano-Christian," meaning "Christian in a pagan way, or with an admixture of paganism."[3] This "pagano-Christian" is one who adheres to a type of Christianity diluted by, or interspersed with, pagan practices. The infiltration of pagan values and forms into Christian churches in America troubles me and has caused me to write this book.

These pages by an American who has spent the greater part of the last thirty years overseas present the reflections of a churchman who loves both his

[1] Harvey Cox, *The Secular City*, Macmillan, New York, 1965, p. 91.
[2] Wayne H. Cowan, ed. *What the Christian Hopes for in Society*, Reflection Book, Association Press, New York, 1957, p. 123.
[3] *Oxford English Dictionary*, Vol. VII, Oxford, Clarendon Press, London, 1961.

church and his country and is concerned over what he sees and senses as he travels in the States. He is also interested in the church and the world. The book is intended for Americans who may be—who should be—equally worried about what is happening to the churches and the culture of our beautiful and bounteous land.

Many are the voices proclaiming that God is dead, that the church is irrelevant beyond repair, and that society is incurably sick. They paint a dismal picture of the organized churches in the "Great Society"—which is beginning to disintegrate before it reaches the peak of its greatness. If one reads the countless books about the plight of the churches on the American scene, he is likely to be enveloped in deep despair. It is not my wish to add to that despair.

My purpose is fourfold. First, I wish to voice my alarm at what I see happening in the life of the churches in America, but also to offer hope. Second, I want to add world perspective to the problem, as well as to any attempted solutions. The magnitude of the question cannot be seen, nor can even semi-valid solutions be offered, until the problem is brought into world focus. Third, I think that confrontation is constructive if done from a positive motivation and in the right spirit. I plan to confront.

Last—a word from a churchman close to the structure of his denomination may give encouragement to young ministers and laymen from many churches who are wrestling with the problem of renewal. Often they feel that those at the center of the structure neither sense their anguish nor hear the voices crying from the rocks.

As I travel about, speaking in American churches, I am often asked, "What do you think of our churches in the States?" There seems to be some apprehension about the reaction of a visitor from overseas. Because there is never time for a long monologue, I have often refrained from giving any specific reply. I do not wish to refrain any longer, however.

It is not unusual for the American missionary abroad to be asked about the position of the churches in his homeland on vital social questions such as race or the war in Vietnam. If he becomes involved in social issues on the overseas scene, he is often reminded of the treatment accorded to minority groups in America.

This book is, in part, a reply to the gibe of Europeans in Africa: "Why don't you go back to America and say or do something about the situation there?"

Very frankly, this book also arises out of personal frustrations that stem from my desire to say something creative and helpful about the life of my own mother church. Usually I do not find any channels through which I can speak candidly. In the structure of the denomination it is assumed that the overseas churchman has nothing pertinent to say about procedures and practices in the American church.

But the times call for candid speech. It is imma-
terial whether the speaker is an American or a Zim-
babwean, provided he feels he has insights that may
be helpful in the mutual struggle for existence. The
time is past in the world—and I trust is passing in
the church—when the acceptability of one's contribution depends upon the passport he carries, the
color of his skin, or the area he represents. As followers of Jesus Christ, we have a divine imperative
to speak boldly in his name and for the sake of his
bride—the Church.

No one can approach a controversial subject of
this type without feeling certain limitations. I have
no desire to be ungracious to the many conscientious Christians to whom I am indebted. Being a
missionary limits one still further in that the whole
missionary enterprise is based on a relationship of
dependence. As one person from overseas said,
"When you Americans pay the bills, it is difficult for
us to speak frankly." Another cautioned, "You must
remember that Americans are highly sensitive to
criticism of any kind." No one likes to be criticized.
I can only hope that my many hosts and hostesses
and innumerable friends, who have been so gracious and generous over the years, will realize how
difficult it is for me to be frank in criticizing a system in which they too have been caught. I beg them
to remember I criticize the *system*, not *persons*. I
covet the continued friendship of those many Christians who are bound in a system that may dull their
witness and limit their stature in Christ. I would,

however, be less than true to them, as well as to myself, if I did not speak out against the growing impotence of the churches in modern society and call attention again to the power that is available if we wish to utilize it.

The fact that I speak from an overseas viewpoint has given me an opportunity to be more objective about the church in America than I could have been had I been more of an integral part of it. The very fact that I live in Africa has made Americans a little less reserved in expressing their thoughts about some of the problems they see in the current structure and practices. An organization man who is leaving soon for overseas is not nearly the threat of one who remains to supervise!

I   •*A Limited Involvement*

I love my church for the spiritual nourishment, the challenge, and the opportunities for service that she has given me. At the same time I am troubled about her because she has grown old, conservative, respectable, and proud. At one time she set out to save the world—and that in one generation. Now she seems more anxious to save her own structure, rigid and worn though it be. At one time she sent out circuit riders to proclaim their faith along the frontiers; now she seems cautious lest she become too involved anywhere.

She may well be anxious about her future, for the moment the church—or any individual or group—becomes self-centered, she begins to write her own epitaph: "She became ill when she grew too exclusive to identify with the poor and socially downtrodden; she worsened because she had no desire to lose herself in service."

But the long night of withdrawal and decline need not claim another victim. The church has done much and can still be relevant and dynamic by getting more involved in the world around her.

Therefore I beg her to gird herself for a new thrust into the whole world.

When I was a boy, the northwest Iowa community in which we lived was a world unto itself. Across the road lived the Witchens, with whom we exchanged threshing and from whom we bought apples to last us through the long cold winter. To the north dwelt the Heldts—tall and pipe-smoking —who came periodically and helped us paint our farm buildings. The Sam Woods, who specialized in Percheron horses, lived directly west of us, and to the east were the loyal Lutheran Zehnders, who raised black Angus cattle and had children my age with whom we went sleighing and one of whom I later dated.

We were surrounded by simple but industrious people whose names indicated their national origins, people we trusted and knew as individuals. Our families shared work, machinery, stories, and common hopes. We children hung May baskets at each other's doors and played hide-and-go-seek together in the moonlight. We rode the same horse-drawn bus to school in the winter, toes tingling from the frost, and played games and cheered each other on. In winter it was basketball; in spring, baseball; in fall, football. But in summer we worked together, all heavily involved on our farms and in the little community on the flat Iowa plains.

My grandchildren's world is not so simple and secure as the one I knew and in which I grew up. My oldest grandchild—a boy of nine—has already lived in Indianapolis, Indiana; Los Angeles, California; Chillicothe, Ohio; Baltimore, Maryland; and is now in Gondar, Ethiopia. The world for this generation is inhabited by people they'll never know intimately. Strangers live in the same line of town houses or even in the same apartment building, perhaps in the apartment next door. On the other hand, others may live thousands of miles away geographically, but today they also are our neighbors, for modern methods of transportation and communication have shrunk our world until it is not much larger than the Lloyd Township of my boyhood. No longer can we count neighbors on our fingers—they have multiplied by the thousands and live in every part of the world. We cannot remain alive spiritually unless our love, evidenced by our involvement, reaches out and embraces these neighbors, wherever they may be. This involvement must include understanding, the sharing of our financial resources, and serving.

We must get to know them, and they us. For too long we have assumed that the learning must be done by others, not by us. Two hundred years ago America was the great melting pot. Our forefathers came up with a single basic culture, and those coming to our shores adjusted to its pattern. We developed an "American way of life," good for a generation living in isolation. But now that the frontiers have disappeared, must all the world go to *our* school? Isn't it just as important for us to learn others' way of life as for them to learn ours? Certainly in the melting pot of the world the American pattern is not going to emerge as the only one worth while.

One of our national problems is our assumption that other peoples accept the same values and strive for the same goals that we do. But each nation, each tribe, even each social group tends to consider the values of its own culture as right and all others as wrong. Last fall in Chicago, African student André dos Santos told me, "For you Americans whatever is not American is erroneous." For too long we have judged others by our own measuring stick, assuming that they do not have one of their own. We need to be aware that as we judge others we are being judged, and the basis for the judgment is not always the same.

An American woman may prize freedom from the responsibilities of the home. An African woman prizes highly her brood of children around her and feels uncomfortable if her back is cold, i.e., if she is not carrying a baby there.

In many societies the volume of business is deliberately limited. Quantity sales are discouraged, for the tax is levied on the gross volume rather than the profits; hence, a small turnover with a higher margin of profit is preferable. Then, too, volume sales might mean going out of business and the loss of location rights, because supplies are limited. In such situations quantity sales are undesirable.

The matter of sharing has great ramifications. Any respectable member of an African tribe would share his possessions with members of his family and tribal group. Therefore the accumulation of wealth does not have the significance it does in Western society. In fact, it may be exceedingly foolish to be known for great possessions, for friends and relatives may move in in order to enjoy the prosperity.

The communal society, with its custom of sharing, does not understand our Western emphasis on achievement and success. Our aggressiveness is offensive to those who have been taught to harmonize their lives with their peers and avoid calling attention to themselves. People whose sharing habit is meaningful find it difficult to understand a system of values emphasizing personal possessions. Our idea that prestige mounts with material acquisitions is absolutely counter to theirs of sharing.

Equally incomprehensible to others is our reluctance to share—especially since it is implicit in the Christian ethic to which we give verbal assent. Sharing, even when there is little to share except the time of day, is very significant for many peoples of the world. As a missionary I have been a recipient of favors that I knew were hard to grant, but to have refused them would have been a rejection of friendship. Sharing and receiving established a bond of fellowship and brought with it a sense of mutual obligation and benefit.

Even work takes on a different aspect when it is viewed from the perspective of the nonacquisitive member of a communal society. He may appear lazy to a Westerner obsessed with ideas of achievement, success, and prestige; but the non-Westerner may really be enjoying a life free from tensions and full of friendships.

A story is told about a government official of Zambia who failed to appear on television as scheduled. It seems that as he sped to the airport to catch a plane, he met three men by the roadside, one of whom had been a childhood friend. Since African etiquette calls for more than a hand wave, the official stopped his car and inquired about the man's health, his family, his crops and livestock. As they chatted, his plane zoomed overhead; it had taken off without him. When Zambian President Kenneth Kaunda learned of the episode and of the wrath of the TV program director, he defended the minister's diplomacy in having chosen the importance of greeting an old friend over catching a plane. Friendship stands near the top of the ladder of African values. Before their traditional culture was disturbed by the Western influence, the ability to live in peace and harmony with one's neighbors meant achieving the highest goal of the community. Making and keeping appointments may be called efficiency in America, but it does not always help in maintaining good personal relationships. It all depends on one's sense of values.

In their interview from Sweden, the four young men who defected from the American Navy in late 1967 appealed to their parents and friends at home to take the blindfolds from their eyes so they could see the world as it is. One of the young men mentioned the church as one of the American institutions obstructing a wider and clearer vision. As the blindfolds are lifted and understanding increases there will be pleasant surprises.

Our American involvement in understanding is quite superficial. We are proud—even egotistical—about what America can offer to the rest of the world. Hundreds of thousands of American tourists have bragged about American art in Florence, American cuisine in Paris, American scenery in Switzerland, and American industry in Western Germany. The American supersalesman is so busy proclaiming the value of his wares that he has little time to learn from others. While we have no reason to be ashamed of the accomplishments of our forefathers, neither have we any reason to assume that we have reached the apex of national development. Europe has given, and continues to give, cultural enrichment, technicians, and scholars to the world. Africa has more than gold and diamonds, copper and chrome. India's Gandhi created the passive resistance movement. The culture of old China is renowned and, though we may find it difficult to think that anything good can come out of modern mainland China, the day will come when it will be advantageous for us to enter into a reciprocal sharing relationship again.

Those with a mind to help need not travel abroad to find opportunities to gain and share understanding. Every day we meet people who are burdened with despair. If only someone had time to listen sympathetically and understandingly! Increasingly, we go to psychiatrists. What is the main help they offer us? Sympathetic understanding of our problems. They listen, probe a bit, then listen again. We begin hesitantly, not sure of the response of this expensive specialist. When we realize, slowly, that someone is really *listening,* our woes pour out.

Members of an affluent society can afford twenty-five to fifty dollars an hour for a listener, but what of those who cannot? A friendly, sympathetic interest in someone whose pent-up emotions are about to explode can accomplish much.

At a church structure meeting in Green Lake, Wisconsin, in November, 1966, Dr. Eugene Smith of the World Council of Churches declared, "If the cry of human agony were caught in one sound wave it would be so powerful as to kill us all."

Many of us go around with heartaches because we cannot find anyone with whom to share our problems. We seek, but everyone seems too busy with his own affairs and uninterested in ours. So we continue to carry our burdens; sometimes we break under them. Understanding others—be they from Timbuctoo, Tunis, or Texas—takes time and energy, but the world *needs* individuals who *care.* We must be willing to go down into the valley with the troubled people, to let them know that they are not alone in their struggle.

Dr. Frank Buchman of Moral Rearmament fame had only one rule to govern him and his followers:

care so deeply for others that among the famished one feels actual hunger, among the shoeless one's feet sting with frostbite on a cold morning. Sargent Shriver expressed it another way when speaking to Board of Missions officials in Denver in January of 1968. He said that if the war on poverty is to be won the affluent members of society must get into the skins of those who are oppressed.

In spite of cultural differences, as we get to know other peoples of the world we shall find them surprisingly like ourselves. They too have been conditioned by their environment and education. They aren't Communists just because they are different from us. Those who live under Communistic or other totalitarian regimes are conditioned unquestionably by the party-line interpretation of events. What is presented to them as fact, we call propaganda; but the essence of personhood binds them to us and us to them. We, too, believe some of our own propaganda. And they may not approve of some of their leaders any more than we approve of some policies foisted upon us by any given government.

We continue to dismiss as questionable hundreds of millions of our neighbors who live outside of America—we don't *know* them. Their patterns of life are different from ours. They speak languages we do not understand. We are not certain of their political inclinations, and because we do not trust them we exclude them from our world, giving them uncomplimentary labels to justify our actions.

Doris Hartman, an intelligent American who

holds a world view, wrote from Hiroshima in August, 1965, "I pray that as Americans we may be able to listen to what Christians in other nations have to say to us instead of dismissing people who differ from us by labeling them as 'Communists' and forgetting them. May we somehow find ways to communicate on a people-to-people level with those in every country whose great longing is to bring up their children in peace."

That we find it difficult to comprehend other peoples does not bother me so much as does the fact that we assume we have no *need* to comprehend them. Our economic strength, hence our military and technological potential, deludes us into a false sense of superiority and security. As we gain understanding of others, we come to appreciate their stature as individuals. We learn *why* they do things differently: climate, calorie intake, conjugal relations, even the cryptozoites (malarial parasites) affect life and behavior patterns.

This understanding is not easily acquired. It is especially important for Americans who go to foreign lands to do some pretrip research. For instance, they should know that in some cultures patterns of behavior require agreement with a guest. Although he may disagree violently with the validity of a statement made by a guest, the gracious non-American host will often give token assent lest he offend his distinguished guests. How many times miscalculations have been made in important matters because the visitor did not seek the answer behind the answer! This does not apply only to those living overseas; it is one of the basic principles of understanding anywhere. The validity of a reply lies not only in the words given but in the totality of the personality of the individual communicating. A verbal "yes" reply can mean a "no" answer or vice versa. It is important to be aware of the feelings behind the words, because people sometimes react more on the basis of their feelings than on the basis of their pronouncements.

Understanding other peoples means more than learning about polite behavior in a given culture. Real involvement requires giving of self; it is all tied up in a gospel that culminated in a cross. *Any kind of deep involvement means some kind of cross.* Is it a fear of the cross that is making our churches more pagan than Christian? There is no detour to take us around the cross if we are to find life. Except a grain of corn falls into the earth and there expends itself in an outburst of new life, it is finished. Life begins at the cross, for it is more than a symbol; it is a reality in the life of each one who gets involved, and the more involved he becomes, the more evident the cross.

We would all do well to read again the Gospels, especially the early chapters that follow the Sermon on the Mount. Immediately after proclaiming his doctrine, Jesus validated his teaching in practice. He became involved, deeply and immediately, in the lives of all kinds of people—lepers, cripples, beggars, prostitutes, wealthy taxpayers, government officials, and the mentally unbalanced. He did not run away to escape involvement, except when his own physical and spiritual resources became so depleted that he needed the isolation of the mountains to recuperate.

The gospel story is one of continuous involvement. God so loved that he gave his son and in that very deed became actively engaged in the affairs of this world. Jesus came, and the record of his public ministry is one of constant and intense participation with all kinds of people in their problems. He gave his disciples the commission of continued involvement in the lives of men and the affairs of nations. We are called to witness through our constructive involvement; this is our heritage as well as our calling.

We need not go to critics of the church to know that we have failed in the quality and quantity of our involvement. As sensitive laymen and pastors we are conscious of our sins of omission. In the face of the American church's potential and opportunities for creative witnessing, who would deny that positive involvement has been far too limited?

But there are bright stars of achievement that shine in the darkness. When world interest started to focus on Africa in 1960—sixteen new nations came into being in that one year alone—my denomination appealed for an accelerated program of training for future African leaders. Of the approximately one million dollars raised, some four hundred and fifty thousand were set aside in a special scholarship fund. More than fifty students from Rhodesia (many with wives and children) went to the States or to Europe for university training. Most of them are now back in Rhodesia; at least 90 per cent are in work directly related to the churches, primarily in important posts in secondary education. The foresight of these American church leaders prevented a radical curtailment of the educational facilities available to present-day African youth in the tormented land of Rhodesia. This overseas educational thrust, although it was beset by administrative difficulties, may well go down in history as one of the most important programs the church has undertaken in Rhodesia. Similar results were obtained for students from other countries as well.

The fact that such a program could be realized only highlights the need for sustained and expanded involvement in Africa and elsewhere. I cannot speak in specific terms of the needs of many other emerging nations of the world, but I am positive that dramatic possibilities exist in almost every land. Too often our affluent Christian society chooses to invest in monuments rather than in men, in bonds rather than in brothers, in yachts rather than in young people.

As an American, I am troubled by our growing reputation for cold apathy to fellow Americans and especially to non-Americans. As a churchman I am aware of what this indifference does to the soul of man as well as its negative influence upon any kind of Christian witness. As a person I deplore this insensibility, for it reveals the extent of our fear of involvement, our egoism, and our selfishness. No one can remain unresponsive to the needs of others without destroying within himself some of the nobleness of his humanity and the essence of his divinity. Our fear of involvement is making us a faceless and a heartless people.

The cause for the lack of creative involvement of the church is difficult to pinpoint. It is easy to blame the pastor, but are we missionaries to blame, perhaps, for the picture we paint? Perhaps because of our presentation, laymen are interested only in saving the souls and healing the bodies of men and not in quickening their minds or restoring their bruised dignity. I believe that our involvement is limited because we have never seen what love, understanding, and insistence on justice (as well as contributions of money) can do for the rejected in our own society and for the masses elsewhere in the rapidly emerging areas of the world.

When a missionary friend visited me recently, we talked about the stewardship of our financial resources. (This man, who lives on a minimal missionary salary, has four children of his own.) When I asked him how Rhodesian African families were finding money to send their children to high school, he replied that the current rural economy was very low and that many bright children were unable to attend because of the lack of educational facilities and of money for tuition and board. As we talked, I learned that this missionary was at that moment helping fourteen African students get through high school. His dedication to a cause and his interest in people reduced his and his family's own standard of living, but it made meaningful sharing possible.

My purpose is not to raise more funds for missions, much as they may be needed. My interest is in people: What may happen to American church members who turn deaf ears to the needs of fellow Christians anywhere? What may be the despairing reaction of Christians who feel themselves rejected?

Idealists in many lands have already repudiated the church. They consider it smug and self-satisfied and hypocritical. They do not reject Christ, only those people who organize themselves into groups in the name of Christ *yet do not follow his teachings or example.*

Christianity is supposed to be a fellowship—but there can be no fellowship without sharing, identifying with, and relating to all of the other members. Geographical areas matter less and less in our world of rapid travel and instantaneous communication, but the church still talks of "overseas" or "foreign" or "underprivileged" constituents. Churches that function like clubs with exclusive memberships, expensive buildings and equipment, and pitying charity for those "outside" should remove the word "Christian" from their vocabulary.

Too general an idea among American church members seems to be that "others" need less than they themselves do. When people think primarily of themselves, forgetting or ignoring the feelings and needs of their fellows, fellowship disintegrates. This is as true in a council of administrators as in the general church. On the other hand, sharing can bring new confidence, new buoyance, new determination, and a new power to achieve.

In the newly independent nations of the world, the rate of progress is going to be amazingly rapid. The Christian people of affluent countries now have an opportunity to share with those in less developed areas. Will the Christian church take this opportunity? It may well be the last. A decade of sustained generosity based on understanding and fellowship could make an idelible impact on the world.

One concrete possibility of sharing exists in the Congo right now. At the time of the nationalist uprising in Angola in 1961, and during the prolonged guerrilla war in the north, between three hundred thousand and a half a million people fled to the Congo. Most of them are Baptists or Roman Catholics or Animists by religion and belong to the Kikongo tribe. Among them also are Methodists, Congregationalists, Adventists, and Plymouth Brethren from other tribal areas. All are refugees in every sense of the word. The local churches are trying to minister to their physical and spiritual needs, but the task is a staggering one since the refugees do not have the economic or physical facilities to do much for themselves.

African children have never had many educational opportunities in Angola because of Portuguese disinterest and official limitations on non-Catholic religious agencies. Little can be done at this time to change the situation in Angola itself, but there is comparative freedom of operation in the Congo—freedom of opportunity to help the psychologically bruised new generation of refugees become responsible adults of tomorrow. How? By establishing middle schools and high schools for the children of the refugees. At the present time there is only token church involvement, because this area is outside the regular work of most American boards of missions.

Another possibility is in northern Mozambique, where the African nationalists are in control of an area nearly as large as the state of Indiana. They welcome assistance in training their people for positions of public service as well as in setting up those services.[1]

A rather unique school is the ten-year-old Women's Training Center (WTC) of the Mindolo Ecumenical Foundation, located near Kitwe, Zambia. WTC was founded to help African women bridge the cultural gap that separates them from their more advanced husbands.

Present-day African men in public life—like many fast-rising, self-made American men—need more from their wives than motherhood and homemaking. The curriculum at WTC has been tailored to meet this need. The forty women living at the

[1] See *Africa Report*, November, 1967.

school (chosen from over four hundred applicants for each five-month term) study family life, hygiene, woman's role in home and community, and youth leadership, as well as basic subjects like sewing, knitting, and baby care.

One course, "The Woman in the Community," offers a wide range of subject material: understanding post office service, opening a savings account, the value of a will and how to write one, understanding rural administration, and glimpses of community life in such places as India, Hong Kong, the Philippines, and the United States.

WTC graduates are the school's best advertisement. (Its most illustrious graduate is the present First Lady of Zambia, Mrs. Betty Kaunda, who puts into practice daily the skills she learned as one of WTC's first students.) Applications are already pouring in for next year. As more and more women go through WTC, there will be an even greater demand for this kind of modern training, done in a Christian environment by qualified and dedicated teachers.

The fact that American economic enterprises extend around the world should make American Christians doubly involved in the lives of those who live far from our suburban homes. But even if our gold bars did not come from the mines around Johannesburg, South Africa, wouldn't we have *some* responsibility for the little black boy in faraway Mozambique whose father spends eighteen months out of twenty-four away from home, mining the yellow dust that makes up those bars?

We are not asked to solve the problems of other people; we are asked only to *be* people—understanding and responsive. (Africans use the word *ubuntu*, similar in meaning to the Latin *humanitas*, to describe that quality of life which distinguishes man from the lower animals.) If we can give ourselves in understanding and sharing, we shall have complied, partially, with the mandates of the gospel and with the expectations of the many who are caught in a dilemma in undernourishment and despondency.

The per capita income of people in India is reported to be less than one thirteenth of the average American income, and that of Brazil about one eighth. Unfortunately the cost of living in those countries does not dip in keeping with income, so many people go undernourished for years and many die of starvation. Those people are our neighbors—Hindus, Muslims, Baptists, Congregationalists, Roman Catholics, Methodists, Episcopalians, Presbyterians, or whatever—and we cannot escape our responsibility to do something about their plight.

In *My Hope for America* President Johnson wrote, "On three continents, in dozens of countries, hundreds of millions of people struggle to exist on incomes of little more than a dollar a week. Many people have less to spend each day on food and on shelter and clothing, on medicine, on all of their needs, than the average American spends at his corner drugstore for a package of cigarettes." [2]

Many people near us could be nearly destitute, but we would not know them personally because our trips to and from suburbia do not pass their doors. As a Michigan friend wrote in his Christmas, 1967, letter, "Detroit has the same conditions as other large metropolitan areas—a deteriorating, overcrowded inner city, with unemployment and seemingly no avenue of escape from the environment of poverty and dismay." In many instances we have abandoned the inner cities. But even though they are physically and psychologically invisible to us, these people *do* exist—just barely, if we compare our monthly salary check with their average yearly income. Their plight is, to quote the Michigan friend again, "the culmination of years of disinterest, mistreatment, and selfishness on the part of us all." Intellectually we know that persons living near us are in need, but we have little emotional understanding for those neighbors—white, black, and coffee-colored—all people for whom Christ died.

Often we think of those outside of our ethnic, social, or national group as "just" Negroes, Japanese, Indians, or hillbillies, but they too are people in whom God has implanted a tremendous potential. This potential develops creatively and constructively or withers away like any unused talent,

[2] Lyndon B. Johnson, *My Hope for America*, Random House, New York, 1964, p. 93.

because it is governed by conditions over which they have little control. I can see them; I can hear them—the hungry of Calcutta, of Caracas, of Watts and Mississippi—and I observe our church potential, our God-given resources for good or evil. How will they be used?

It is easy to find excuses for noninvolvement. We can go back to the curse of Ham and claim (as do the Reformed Churches of South Africa) that racial origin prevents us from bringing the impoverished and depressed into a meaningful fellowship. We can bolster ourselves with myths about "the happy poor" and the "joys of the simple life." We can resort to the concept of prosperity for the righteous and impoverishment for the evildoer, as do many fundamentalists. We can smugly cite statistics showing that no matter how many Americans live a substandard existence their plight is paradise compared to the poor of the lands from which their great grandparents came.

I have heard my colleagues affirm again and again that ministers and laymen are loyal to the church. In this I rejoice. Sometimes I wonder to what church they refer? Loyalty to Christ's church reminds us to do something about the starving mothers trying to nurse famished infants at flat, dry breasts, as we nibble half-interested on T-bone steaks and Idaho baked potatoes smothered in sour cream. It brings into focus shivering, ill-clad children as we worship in our well-heated sanctuaries. Loyalty to Christ's church must pull one from his comfortable pew to the door of the needy in his own community. Loyalty to Christ's church must take one into the "African townships" of Salisbury and the "bairros" of Luanda before going to the Wankie and Kruger game reserves on African safari.

On my last trip to America I spent a week with my son and his family in Ethiopia. Leaving Asmara in an Ethiopian jet plane, I flew over the Sahara at thirty thousand feet. Even so, I could see the glistening white ribbon of the Nile River far below. On either side was the monotonous, yellow-brown sand, hardly shifting on a quiet, sunny Saturday. As the plane approached Cairo, narrow canals angled off to the right and left of the Nile, carrying water into what once had been a desert. Now the green vegetation and abundance of the breadbasket of Egypt appeared. As the water of the Nile loses itself in the sands of the Sahara, new life comes forth to sustain a nation.

In many an American church the water of life is confined to the narrow limits of the church membership, while all around are the parched and thirsty who need that life-giving water. We must breach the thick walls so that the fountain of life may be available to all who want to drink.

I love my native America, but I cry out in anguish over her lack of concern, her self-centered smugness. Can't the gulf be bridged between her affluence and the world's need? Can't we give, to bring modest comfort, health, and sufficiency for all?

I love my church, but I covet for her the involvement that leads to Jerusalem—and Golgotha. Only in a total involvement will there be a cross and from the cross a breaking forth into dynamic new life.

II   *A Frozen Structure*

Most people of this generation are accustomed to change. Our mode of living and methods of transportation and communication have all altered radically during the past quarter of a century. Farming as I knew it in my boyhood has virtually disappeared; most American farms are now highly mechanized. Industrial procedures have been stepped up and refined; businesses have such far-flung empires that mobility has become a way of life. In many communities at least one third of the residents move every five years or oftener.

We have come to understand that changes take place whether we want them or not. We live in that kind of world. Long-established patterns of life are called into question. No institution can escape the challenge of an era of change. In order to survive, we human beings adapt to changing conditions. So must social institutions.

While certain changes have been going on in America, even more revolutionary ones have been taking place in other parts of the world. Up until now, our changes have been more complete and have taken place with greater rapidity.

Twelve years ago the enormous, wealthy, diverse continent of Africa had only four independent nations. At last count there were thirty-nine. They are striving to develop independently in keeping with African cultural patterns, modified by world contacts. Internal and external influences change these patterns from time to time. American and European churches can be proud of their contribution to a progressive and generally peaceful social revolution in Africa. We are seeing changes take place on a scale never before seen in human history, with a minimum of destructive violence. And what is happening in Africa has already taken place in Asia.

Social changes come more slowly in Latin America than in Asia and Africa. There the church opposed change, as it did also in southern Europe. The very fact that most of the Latin-American countries have been independent for many decades—even centuries—has made it more difficult for the social revolution to operate effectively. In Africa and Asia part of the dynamic change has come with nationalism and the movement toward political independence.

The transformation that has taken place in other parts of the world has provided greater stimuli for change in America. It has provided new areas of investment, new opportunities for industrial expansion, and greater opportunities to serve through the traditional church agencies plus new governmental ones such as the Peace Corps, AID, and other benevolent programs. Influences which have come either directly or indirectly from the rest of the developing world have militated against stagnation in American society.

The emergence of the new nations in Africa and Asia has done much to stimulate the civil rights movement in the States. The American Negro, for the first time, is beginning to take pride in his origin and culture. As he watches Africans, some of whom have been exposed to Western culture for less than a hundred years, direct their own affairs, he receives an impetus to assert his personality—to become a full member of the "Great Society."

Although we Americans have made great strides in technology, we are woefully behind in social relations—conservative, even reactionary. We welcome new artifacts: air-conditioned cars, electric carving knives and toothbrushes, automated bank accounts and bills that warn, "Do not bend, staple, or mutilate." Yet, what do we do about our slums, our underprivileged, our stigmatized social outcasts?

In September of 1966, Dr. Charles Edward Fuller of Scarritt College in Nashville, Tennessee, stressed the religious inertia that affects our social life.

It is quite likely that among some of the shouting Christians in some communities some of the most vocal are those in a new car, with the latest model appliances in their "homes of tomorrow," wearing the latest style clothing, sporting the most way-out hairdo, and avoiding anything out-of-date. But in the realm of their religious life they prefer to sing "What was good enough for my father is good enough for me" as they denounce every change they see in religious thought and life about them.

Robert Spike once told of a kindly nun who flew from Jackson, Mississippi, during the civil rights struggle there. As she talked to her seatmate the nun decried the presence of Northern white students in Mississippi. Although she sympathized with the purpose of the students—aiding voter enrollment—and did not question their dedication, she felt that they should not "stir up" the local white racial supremacists because violence might occur.[1] The nun's reaction is not an unusual one. She preferred a calm lake, even though polluted, to a roiled one. Her feeling that it is worse to create turmoil than to continue to endure the injustices of past centuries is shared by many pietistic Christians who seek tranquillity at any price. This attitude can be found in parts of the New Testament, but it is not the *whole* gospel. Christians *should* be crying for a meaningful opportunity to engage in the struggle to eliminate injustices and to bring society into closer harmony with the will of God. What does the Lord require of us but to do justly, to love mercy, and to walk humbly with him? Christians need to shed their reputations for seeking peace at any price—if peace means leaving an evil, unjust *status quo* undisturbed. What they should be crying for is

[1] Robert W. Spike, *The Freedom Revolution and the Churches*, Association Press, New York, 1965, p. 124.

a meaningful opportunity to eliminate injustices and to bring society into closer harmony with the will of God.

One of the great needs of the church today is the development of a theology of confrontation. How does the devoted and awakened Christian within the church express his disapproval of evils in the *status quo* in a gracious yet convincing way? Mere requests for consideration are ignored. Logic is silenced by tradition. Insistence on being heard is counteracted by a thinly veiled threat against "troublemakers." In the end the only way for the conscientious Christian to make himself heard is to adopt the stance of the determined reformer by challenging the guardians of the *status quo*. The power within the privileged establishment always reacts negatively to suggestions of change.

Jesus experienced this conservatism in his day. "It has been said" was followed by "but I say unto you." No longer was it "an eye for an eye and a tooth for a tooth"; rather, the law of love was to prevail. But the establishment would not listen to the new ideas of religious relevance. In the end Jesus set the pattern that was to be followed by most reformers to this day—the use of creative moral force to challenge the guardians of the traditions. How much better it would be if there could be a dialogue in which dissident individuals were able to express themselves!

On the southern African scene, the inability of African nationalist leaders to break through the structure into creative dialogue with the minority white political leaders is the frustrating stumbling block. Dr. Antonio de Oliveira Salazar of Portugal, Mr. Ian Smith of Rhodesia, and Prime Minister John Vorster of South Africa appear afraid to enter into dialogue with African leaders. The political structures are so rigid that they cannot bend without breaking. No creative exchange of ideas is possible.

This leaves little alternative to the people except to remain in submissive subjection to the injustices within the current political structure or to challenge it through organized resistance. Where no penetration of the structure in positive cooperative interchange is possible, negative resistance (leading eventually to a positive challenge of position through violence) is the only alternative they can see.

One of the tragedies of southern Africa lies in the fact that creative dialogue could have been carried on peacefully, but the minority groups in power refused to give an opening for talks. Thus, rejected and frustrated nationalists, who feel responsibility for their people's future, turn to violence as the only way to get out from under harsh domination.

To return to the American church scene, if there is rebellion within the ranks of the church—as there is—the guardians of the structure need to open the doors for dialogue. People in general are so constituted that they do not rebel unless they think they have just cause. Often the opportunity to express their grievances will suffice to release the pent-up frustrations and will permit them to view their world with greater objectivity. They may well have suggestions that are valid and good for their society.

Often the most creative people become the most frustrated when they encounter rigidity in the structure. Their integrity and creativity drives them into open rebellion when they encounter the frigid, unresponsive, and authoritarian superiors who guard the ramparts. They press for change and take their chances of survival. The less creative, less dynamic, less imaginative will conform to the *status quo,* for in conformity they find protection.

We all know that it is easier to adjust to change physically than to do so emotionally or psychologically. We resist church integration, for instance, because we may have to move to the right or the left of our accustomed position in order to let new elements come into our fellowship. For this same reason we do not like to admit large new elements into our own social strata or to change our order of worship. We do not want our Sunday routine upset; we don't want to be disturbed, we want to be "inspired"; we want to come away from church with a warm feeling. Let our ministers have enough surprises to keep us awake, but let them also be predictable. Let the old practices and phrases suffice, even though they may no longer be meaningful. We have become accustomed to them and that makes them good.

Any change requires understanding. We need to see where we are going and why. If we do not receive that information we react negatively and emotionally. We have absorbed most of our culture patterns automatically because they have been bequeathed to us and we do not question them. We are like the bride who always cut a ham in two before putting it on to boil. When her husband asked her why she cut it in two, she replied that it cooked better that way. When pressed for a more explicit reason she could not give any. But the next time her mother came to visit she asked her the reason for cutting a ham before boiling it.

"Don't ask me why; it's just done that way," replied her mother. Then, after a moment's thought, she added, "It was Granny who taught me to cut hams; why not ask her?"

When the girl next visited her grandmother, the answer was simply, "When I was a girl, our pots weren't big enough to hold a whole ham."

So do our traditions grow. We see no reason to change what Granny did sixty years ago. But those whose eyes are not blinded, whose ears are not stopped, whose minds are not set, whose spirits are not controlled—those with vision have plenty of reasons to support growth and change.

If we benefit from the *status quo* we are likely to oppose change, also, and the degree of opposition will depend upon the benefits we receive. Strong compensation of some kind may be necessary to overcome our natural inertia, bolstered by our benefits.

If gradual change does not occur in keeping with the times, one of two things usually happens—stagnation or revolution. Stagnation usually takes place only in those areas of the world that are cut off from a ready stream of outside stimuli. In times past, stagnation was most evident in some of the isolated hill, and mountainous regions of the United States and on a wide continental scale in Africa.

For centuries Africa had been cut off from the rest of the world by the composition of her terrain and by her climate, which produced many insect-borne diseases. Her rivers were not navigable to the sea; her culture did not encourage change from within. Now and then individuals of personal magnetism and consequent power, such as Chaka, Lobengula, or Queen Njinga, reached a position from which they could introduce reform.

Today stagnation is almost a thing of the past. As modern methods of communication and transportation have interlinked the world, rebellion and revolution have become more and more common in those areas where gradual change is thwarted. Change is written into the very order of the universe. If it doesn't take place gradually, it usually breaks out in radical revolt.

If a social system ceases to function logically, violence may be the only way to dislodge the groups that think they benefit from the present order. Only recently has mankind been confronted with a situation in which failure to move forward wisely could mean the destruction of the entire world. There is growing support, therefore, for radical changes that may help to create conditions in which human society can survive.

My desire is to see some kind of framework in which those individuals and groups who feel frustrated by barriers within and without the church can confront successfully their fellow men who erected or who now support those barriers. If tensions and frustrations cannot find a channel through which they may be expressed openly and freely, they can become subversive and later break out into destructive action.

Under the leadership of the late Dr. Martin Luther King, Jr., the Southern Christian Leadership Conference has been a creative element in the American civil rights struggle. Even though Dr. King's dynamic leadership was abruptly terminated by his tragic death, it is to be hoped that those on whom his mantle has fallen will continue the program of nonviolent but direct confrontation. If existing injustices are not corrected and channels for immediate change established, tensions will multiply and soon break loose in uncontrollable fury. Every effort must be made to help existing tensions come to the surface so that they can be dealt with in an atmosphere of social concern—not because of Dr. King's death, but because it is right.

In the light of the need for constant renewal,

adjustment, and change, what about the structures of our churches? Here we find change and adjustment to the new only at the point of absolute necessity. In general, the structures remain rigid, highly traditional, tightly controlled, barren, and cold.

As individuals, the older we get the less flexible we become. So, too, the more seasoned the church structure, the more rigid it tends to become. Whenever an organization is controlled by people over sixty years of age, with the real seat of power moving upward toward the seventy-year level and beyond, a great deal of flexibility cannot be expected.

Traditional culture patterns of African society are similar to church structures. Old people were venerated and listened to—the older and more experienced a man was, the greater the tribal authority vested in him. At times even departed spirits were called upon to settle matters. When ancestral spirits are consulted, you may be sure they will not advocate innovations that would make them insecure in their own milieu any more than the fathers of the church are going to seek out patterns that would alter their positions!

Flexibility of structures—in the church and in African society—can be achieved by shifting the balance of power from the venerable silver-haired saints to the reckless young. We old people strive to keep the organization intact by maintaining the *status quo;* young men and women with vision and inspiration are the ones who must lead the way to change.

The older generation's conservatism has always been—and probably always will be—a thorn in the flesh of younger, more imaginative people. By the time many people get into the structures, they are so exhausted that the best they can do is gravitate toward the center and await their seniority, senility, or both.

Structures tend to set and harden, like cement. When they set, it is difficult to penetrate them with any progressive revelation of truth. In such a rigid setup a revelation of the will of God is no longer desirable, lest too fresh and dynamic a visitation of the Holy Spirit crack, bend, or damage the carefully preserved fixed system.

Church systems have a tendency to become firm in their rigidity; they become frozen. Jesus had his problems with frozen systems of belief, as did Martin Luther, who broke away from the Church of Rome because of the rigidity of the structure of that day and its effect on his faith. Had there been more flexibility, John Wesley might well have kept his flock within the Anglican fold, and William Booth's Salvation Army might have become the Christian Social Concerns Committee of United Methodism!

Our heritage from the past deposits both good and bad at the feet of each successive generation. Today Christians inherit mind-set and ecclesiastical patterns that burden them with the prejudices and faulty structures of the past. Maintaining traditions is not an exclusive prerogative of Roman Catholics.

This tendency toward traditionalism was made

obvious in the adoption of both the Methodist Articles of Religion and the Evangelical United Brethren Confession of Faith in the new United Methodist Church. In spite of attempts to rewrite the two credal statements and unite them in one up-to-date statement, as John Wesley did when he took beliefs from the Church of England and gave them to Methodists in America, we of this generation's structure decided to maintain intact two heritages from one theological past.

The United Methodist Church is a *world* church in this period of history, but Article XXIII of the Articles of Religion still states:

> The President, the Congress, the general assemblies, the governors, and the councils of state as the delegates of the people, are the rulers of the United States of America, according to the division of power made to them by the Constitution of the United States and by the constitution of their respective states. And the said states are a sovereign and independent nation, and ought not to be subject to any foreign jurisdiction.[2]

What a creedal statement for a *world* church coming into being in 1968! To expect Methodists of Mozambique, Hong Kong, Bolivia, and more than forty other countries to ascribe to an article that deals with American politics, not religion, is ludicrous. Maintaining this statement, which should never have been included in the original Articles,

[2] *The United Methodist Church: The Plan of Union* (1967), p. 27. The Methodist Publishing House, Nashville, Tenn.

preserves traditions that may be meaningful to only a few in one national segment of the new world church, a segment that is numerically and financially the strongest.

Within the structures themselves, fairly firm control keeps the majority inarticulate. Usually a vocal 5 per cent does 95 per cent of the talking. This 5 per cent does not necessarily make decisions, but they are the front men; they exert influence. No pecking system of barnyard fowls is better formulated or more rigidly enforced than the right to speak in the councils of the churches. At any meeting of a World Council, a National Council, a General Assembly, a General Conference, most of the speaking is done by the few. This does not mean that others have nothing worthwhile to say, or that they would not contribute if they were given a chance. Certain people who have a combination of position, know-how, aggressiveness, and seniority simply demand the floor and maintain it as their private platform.

In *World Outlook* (December 6, 1966) Arthur J. Moore, Jr., gave his observations on the 1966 Methodist General Conference:

> It is more clear at each succeeding General Conference that the machinery and procedure of the General Conference itself have become demonic. It may be true, as often observed, that the Holy Spirit can work outside structures. It is less clear how much harder it is for Him to work inside the present one. Watching the complicated parliamentary wrangling meant to prevent delegates voting on an issue, who

can confidently proclaim that we are showing forth the Gospel? [3]

In September of 1966, the exclusively white Anglo-Saxon nominating committee of the World Methodist Council reported its slate of nominees for the Executive Committee for the quinquennium 1966–71—composed of forty-eight British and American members and twenty-four members from all the rest of the world. It still left an area nearly as large as the United States unrepresented—all of Africa between the Limpopo River and the Equator.

During the previous quinquennium the Executive Committee had been made up of thirty-six Americans, eighteen Britons, and fourteen from the rest of the world. Most of the Americans and all of the Britons were white, and of the non-Anglo-Saxon group at least half were Caucasians. This former committee had one South African member, a Caucasian—despite the fact that the church there is predominantly African. On the new committee, South Africa is represented by *two* Caucasians. Although both of these members are of recognized stature, many other men and women of potential could have served ably and could have added the common touch and color that the World Methodist Council structures so badly need. But structures have a way of self-perpetuation in tightly controlled traditional forms.

[3] Arthur J. Moore, Jr., *World Outlook* editorial, December 6, 1966, p. 6.

Structures also can become shelters against creative thinking, which we often refer to as criticism.
Roman Catholic clergy may be even more subject to
ivory-tower dwelling than are Protestants, who
usually have parsonage wives to keep them in the
midst of reality. Daniel Callahan, in *Honesty in the
Church*, states that within the Roman Catholic fold
"it is a common quip that once a priest is appointed
bishop he will never again hear the truth." [4]

Friends, admirers, office seekers do their best to
keep any person who holds a position of power in a
constructive and optimistic frame of mind. There
must be no sagging of the ego; all thinking must be
positive if power is to be creative. Thus, as the fa-
vored one moves into the power structures of the
church, a protective curtain of unreality is drawn
around him.

Some of my colleagues may say that I am both
unfair and unrealistic. It is true that brickbats do
occasionally find their mark behind the curtain of
admiration, but, on the whole, respect is given both
to the individual and to the position he holds.

On the other hand, those who hold real grievances refrain from expressing them at times, not so
much out of a sense of fear as out of a reluctance to
impose themselves on their seniors and superiors.
Sometimes they fail to recognize that confrontation
is not necessarily negative; if it is done in a spirit of

[4] Daniel Callahan, *Honesty in the Church*, Charles Scribner's
Sons, New York, 1965, p. 85.

humility and mutual interest, it can be very creative.

Some structure people do not want to listen to
what the outsider tries to communicate—even for
their own good. It may be that they are so saturated
with meetings that they fail to hear even what they
say to each other. There are so many meetings that
often those who attend have no time to think about
the implementation of resolutions passed at previous meetings. This tendency of professional
conference-goers to forget their own resolutions
was alluded to by Allan Brockway. "The crucial test
of the Geneva Conference's accomplishment, however, must wait until the day Christians and
churches begin to embody the faith they pronounce
on at conferences." [5]

Most groups tend to be more insensitive to the
needs of people than do the individuals that com-
prise the group. The more isolated the group, the
more insensitive its members become. It is easier to
imbed the onus of insensitivity and inactivity in a
structure than to bear it personally. If one can share
the onus with others, it may not be troublesome
personally; commit it to a committee—that's an effective way of killing it! The desire of various elements to "stick together" often makes the church
inarticulate or, at best, weak and ineffectual. Structures usually support one another, as do members

[5] Allan R. Brockway, *Concern*, September 15, 1966, p. 2.

within them. Thus they are often insensible to the needs of individuals or minority groups.

Because of the rigidity, insensitivity, and ineffectiveness of church structures, many people say they must all go. Emotionally, I am often ready to agree with them. Then I hear that such weaknesses are all mistakes and that those in power are most anxious to listen to all shades of opinion—even to what the Holy Spirit may be trying to say. I take heart and wait expectantly when I read the words of Dr. Tracey K. Jones, Jr., confirming that my church "is committed to the re-examination of its life and a change in its structure." [6] If this openness to change is real, we can look forward to a new and creative era in the history of the church.

[6] Quoted in address by Bishop Harold R. Heininger at Green Lake, Wisc. COSMOS Consultation, November 1966.

III   *A Fragmented Witness*

Because the churches on the American scene are badly fragmented, the Christian witness is tragically weakened. If the power of the gospel is not sufficiently strong to hold believers together in unity, what does it have to offer to unbelievers?

The world is always observant, and it cries, "Physician, heal thyself!" when it notices an apparent illness in the body of Christ. Unfortunately not all church members are troubled by the divisions within Christendom. Many pagan or pseudo Christians enjoy some of the diluted benefits of organized churches without realizing that anything is amiss. It has always been this way, they feel, and it will continue so indefinitely. This relaxed, lukewarm "Christian" has little interest in the outreach of the gospel into society and the world. He is not worried that the cutting edge of the Christian witness is dulled and ineffective.

Other so-called Christians have not considered the sin of schism seriously and have lost sight of the nature of the church. They have abandoned one denominational structure for personal reasons, set out on their own, and zealously established new patterns very similar to the denominational ones they have just left.

A third group, which Ralph Lord Roy calls "apostles of discord,"[1] tries deliberately to disturb any existing harmony in the established churches. With the seeds of divisiveness thus being deliberately sown, there is little wonder that denominations in America now number nearly three hundred.

Inside the churches there is a fourth group of sincere Christians who have not really thought about the meaning of *unity in Christ*. They are good people, sensitive to the leading of the Holy Spirit, and they are eager to follow in obedience. However, they have never seriously considered the disastrous results of our disunity, nor have they felt a challenge to fellowship with all believers. When such a call is given, and the basis for it firmly established in the Scriptures, I believe they will give a positive response.

Older, established churches often place much of the responsibility for the disunity within American denominations on the "evangelicals" or "Pentecostals." J. Marcellus Kik wrote in *Ecumenism and the Evangelical:*

History does reveal that at times evangelical denominations, although in agreement on the vital doctrines of the Christian faith, have viewed each other as rival kingdoms struggling for the souls of men. A

[1] Ralph Lord Roy, *Apostles of Discord*, Beacon Press, Boston, 1953, p. 374.

bitter and partisan spirit refused to acknowledge that they were brothers in Christ. Each, on occasion, has sought to ruin the other on the pretext of serving the Lord.[2]

But one must never think that liberal Christians are free from the spirit of dissension and divisiveness. At times they have been extraordinarily uncharitable in their attacks upon each other, especially upon those who maintain a more traditional position.

We do not need to go to books and scholars to learn of the broken witness that exists in many communities throughout the United States and, for that matter, throughout the world. We find it in our own communities and in our own denominations. In pioneer days there was a very real need for new houses of worship. The effectiveness of the witness depended upon going out to where people lived. That initial coverage was well done—often tragically overdone.

Liberal, Missouri, is an example; and it is probably not too different from other towns and communities in rural America or, indeed, from many large cities. A local pastor in Liberal told me that there is a church for approximately every hundred people. He said almost everyone who worships must pass one or two other churches before he finds the one of his choice. No longer need one seek a place in

[2] J. Marcellus Kik, *Ecumenism and the Evangelical*, Presbyterian and Reformed Publishing Co., Philadelphia, 1958, pp. 132–133.

which to worship; he may often just attempt to find
the church least likely to disturb his prejudices!
According to a sign at the edge of town, Liberal has
a population of 612. It has six established congregations with their own buildings: a Methodist, a
Christian, a Southern Baptist, a Church of Christ,
and two Churches of God—one based on "proph-
ecy" and the other emphasizing "holiness." In addition, the town has a few Mormons, Christian
Scientists, and Seventh-Day Adventists, and the
surrounding fairly rich farming area has Free Will
Baptist Churches.

Such duplication of churches means there is
excessive and wasteful competition in order to keep
alive. This in turn creates hostile attitudes among
the so-called "Christian" people of a small community.

The present outreach to the world is, of course,
affected by the lack of unity seen in such communities as Liberal. As the churches responded to the
call of mission, the missionaries took overseas with
them their patterns of division and their ideas of
exclusiveness. These divisions have been maintained by different patterns of support and economic control, at times unconscious but nonethe-
less real. Even the prestige patterns enjoyed by
sending agencies in their home countries have become rooted hedges of separation on the mission
field. Thus, the Anglicans usually expect and get
privileges in British spheres of influence overseas.
Roman Catholic churches enjoy special privileges

in Belgian, Portuguese, Spanish, and Italian spheres. Lutherans, by the same token, flourish in areas of former German influence. When missionaries have tried to erase the lines of division among the younger churches, they have been resisted both at home and abroad. At home there is resistance to new patterns because they create problems of readjustment; in the younger churches there is fear that they are being used as guinea pigs in an experiment the mother church is not willing to try in her own back yard.

Once divisions have been established it is not easy to revise them in keeping with divine revelation and with trends of a more enlightened day. Alexander Campbell called the divisions among Christians "a horrid evil" and launched a group called the Disciples in an attempt to bring about Christian unity. It, too, became a denomination (now known as The Christian Church) and added to the sickness which it is still trying to heal.

Critics of the church are quick to point out evidence of disunity, and the faithful are embarrassed. They realize that a fellowship united in worship and service would impress the world, but a church that denies or rejects the gift of fellowship and unity will not make a constructive impact upon the world.

African youth are quick to recognize that something is amiss in a divided church. More than once students have asked me to explain the causes for the divisions within the Christian church. In itself, this has not been hard to do, but bringing outside divisions to Africa and continuing competitiveness in an age of enlightenment is most difficult to justify.

After Zambia became independent in 1965, one of the first steps taken by the church leaders was to unite. Within six months, four denominations or missions came together to form the United Church of Zambia. This could happen in Zambia more easily than in the United States because the traditions of the past are less entrenched among the newer churches than among the historic ones. This makes for greater flexibility and quicker responses, although nowhere is change easy. In a country that has achieved her independence after a comparatively short but intense struggle, however, there is little comprehension of the delaying action that might require a decade, or even a century to arrive at an understanding among Christians.

Why are there so many divisions in the church? And what are the reasons for the continuing fragmentation? At least four causes of disunity are easily discernible:

Our inheritance: Most of the major religious groupings were brought to America by our forefathers. Each brought certain religious knowledge, practices, and preferences in worship. Sometimes these practices were changed, but most people tried to settle in a community of like-minded individuals if possible. Thus a common pattern of worship developed and was carried on to new settlements during the westward trek. Basically, the religious practices of Europe were transferred to America. Those modifications necessary to satisfy our new status as a country of independent people were made—Lutherans lost bishops; Methodists acquired some; Anglicans made fewer modifications, retained their bishops, but changed the name of their church to Episcopal. Unfortunately the political melting pot, which made Americans of all immigrants, did not seem to operate in the field of religion.

Human factors: Sometimes fragmentation has been caused by the rigidity of those in authority, as exemplified by the rise of both Methodism and the Salvation Army in England. At times an ambitious but immature youth who wanted to get ahead faster than was permitted by the structure of his denomination bolted and started his own church. Others left their churches out of a sense of offended pride at having been discharged from their responsibilities. Egoism, combined with a desire for authority, caused some to separate themselves; those who crave power can be found in both the liberal and evangelical camps. Undoubtedly personal ambition contributed to fragmentation.

In South Africa the restrictive political situation is probably responsible mainly for the painful fragmentation of the church. No fewer than two thousand sects and denominations exist in that land of apartheid. Only in the field of religion can non-Caucasians find an outlet for their leadership.

Ignorance: It is not an easy matter to discover the will of God—to understand the divine voice as it comes to us in the early hours of the morning after an evening session with a rigid and unreasonable superior or a church board. Our own desires may cause us to misinterpret the leading of the Holy Spirit, especially if we are not well versed in the Scriptures. Historically, one may think he can see the hand of God at work in the formation of new religious bodies, but the proliferation of our time seems to meet no spiritual or practical purpose.

Theological differences: Because of the latitude of theological beliefs in many of the major denominations, this reason does not seem to be based on reality, although it is often given as a cause of fragmentation. If one cannot find sufficient latitude in his own church, there are nearly three hundred denominations already in existence in the United States. Surely at least one of these must have theological beliefs similar to those of the dissenter. Often we appear to make our decisions and then try to find theological or scriptural justification.

The unity theme—the imperative of oneness—abounds in the New Testament, especially in the Gospel of John and in the writings of St. Paul: ". . . that they may be one"; "One Lord, one faith, one baptism"; "All of us, united with Christ, form one body, serving individually as limbs and organs to one another." Different forms of worship, varied church structures, creeds, and sacraments, need not impede us in serving the Lord in the spirit of unity—unity of the spirit as well as organic unity. If the former is realized, the latter will follow. Some of

the most pietistic individuals and groups fail to realize that, as one becomes part of the true vine, the
common sustaining life in Christ unites one with all
those clinging to other branches. All are nourished
by the same sustaining spiritual sap, which brings
unity among the branches and thus to the whole
vine.

The vine allegory simply illustrates what Jesus
taught in his summary of the commandments:
Upreach to God in love brings about an outreach to
man in fellowship and concern. This outreach was
one of the signs of the early church; this fellowship
in love provided the cutting edge of the Christian
witness—"behold these Christians, how they love
one another"—regardless of race, class, or national-
ity.

According to the Scriptures and to our experience, this new life in Christ will develop an inclusive fellowship among those who have the same
Source for their spiritual existence, the same confidence, the same purpose, the same hope. In Christ a
new life begins in connection with all others who
have the same anchorage. Jesus Christ wills his
church to be of one mind, spirit, and life; only then
can it be one in witness.

If unity be the will of God, obedience to that will
demands that we alter the man-made direction of
the churches and bring them into the central position of God's purpose. When that will is made
known, either we take ourselves out of the fellowship of those united in Christ or, in obedience, we

respond and walk in the light that has come our way.

Times have changed. The rugged individualist is fast disappearing, and geographical frontiers have shrunk. New frontiers may well lie in deeper understanding of both the gospel and of man himself, requiring a unified approach to the total man and total society.

The various boards of missions have been responsive to the new unified approach overseas. Today single denominations rarely undertake new projects if they can get other Christian forces to unite with them in a common approach. The unified witness in Nepal is an excellent example of utilization of denominational resources for a common thrust into the non-Christian world. Governments often accept such joint service projects more readily than weak and competitive individual denominational witness.

Because of our divisiveness, Roman Catholics in Angola were disdainful of Protestants. Officialdom there was reluctant to deal with more than one Protestant agency in any given area. The various denominations working in Angola did not want organic unity, but they were willing to become functionally united in order to put forward their common cause to the government. The fellowship thereby created meant much to each Protestant Christian, and it is a step toward an organic union of believers.

Before the formation of the Congo Protestant

Council in the Congo, the multiplicity of agencies —each clamoring for an opportunity to carve out its own small sphere of religious thinking—was incomprehensible to authorities steeped in the Roman Catholic tradition. Catholicism, despite a certain sharpness of conflict among its wide range of orders, has an over-all organization that represents controls and disciplines. Divided Protestantism has had no such representation and discipline, much to the confusion of the new convert trying to understand the real nature of the church.

The current tendency to strengthen the existing Christian councils in Africa and Asia has led to the undertaking of new projects in the name of evangelical Christianity (if not that of united Christendom) rather than in a denominational name. For example, since its formation three years ago the Christian Council in Rhodesia—where Utopia is still far distant—has employed a part-time youth worker and a missionary for a joint approach in urban areas. A new teacher-training college, while not under direct administration of the Council, has its blessing and is being built to serve a region rather than a single denomination as are other church-training schools. A third project, still on paper, is a hostel for working girls in Salisbury. These new ventures in ecumenical witnessing are an encouraging step toward the future.

For over a decade we in Africa have been training our ministers and other full-time church workers jointly. Although this generation of churchmen has not yet reached places of maximum influence within the denominations, the joint training effort prepares the way for a more common witness in the years ahead. The establishment of *more* denominational theological seminaries here in the States seems to be a move contrary to reason and to the spirit of our times.

There are signs, however, of a brighter tomorrow. In 1966, the Christian university students took a creative and prophetic step when they formed the University Christian Movement. This new movement, which brings together groups as widely separated as Quakers and Roman Catholics, unites most of the denominational university groups. Is this a foretaste of what might happen on national and world scenes if youth had a determining voice in the affairs of churches?

Even the elders, however, are not all asleep! The Consultation on Church Union, which began early in this decade, seems to be gathering strength. According to news releases, seminaries in Boston, Washington, D.C., and elsewhere are forming cluster institutions or joint centers of learning, caring for theological students from all cooperating denominations. In Boston the cluster consists of seven seminaries, which until now have each functioned separately. Together they make up the new Boston Theological Institute, which brings into cooperation four Protestant and three Roman Catholic seminaries.

Who knows what the future will bring forth? But

if young men and women are trained together in an atmosphere of mutual respect—even for individuals who differ sharply with them on points of doctrine and church polity—the ecumenical age will have come nearer. Conviction is growing—in the cities and in conservative rural areas, in America and overseas, among youth and less flexible adults —that the Holy Spirit is leading us to make our witness to our *oneness in Christ*. Bishop James K. Mathews of Boston evaluates this movement toward Christian unity as "one of the most important developments in the whole church in our time. The universality and simultaneity of the movement is, to my mind, a testimony to its being the work of God."

If this be of God, who can resist it?

IV ❧•*An Exclusive Fellowship*

One July Sunday in 1964, William James Humbane, my African secretary and driver, came to worship at the church where I was guest preacher—Wesley Methodist Church in Rusape, Rhodesia. He had barely seated himself before the head usher asked him to leave. Humbane did so at once and without protest. Shortly afterwards, Dr. Morgan Johnson, an American missionary from Georgia who had witnessed the African's arrival and departure, also left. Later, the pair—the white Southern missionary and my black secretary—returned to the sanctuary and worshiped together in a back pew. During the same service two other African men, one a reporter, entered the sanctuary and remained to worship.

Repercussions from the congregation were almost immediate, I was told in some detail later. Right after the service, the head usher and a number of other members asked the pastor to call a congregational meeting to discuss the composition of the fellowship at Wesley Church.

Wesley was a new church, built at considerable sacrifice by its Caucasian congregation, who lived in and around Rusape. Many of its members had migrated to Rhodesia from South Africa to settle in that rich farming region. Socially and politically Rusape was known as a stronghold of conservatism, and Rhodesian Front party leader Ian Smith received strong support from the community in general—including members of Wesley congregation. Many had been brought up to believe in separate development of the races, in America known as segregation, in South Africa, as apartheid.

When the pastor (who, incidentally, was a retired university professor visiting his missionary son and family in Africa) called the meeting to order, the discussion was lively. Members of the congregation were sharply divided on the nature of their fellowship. Should Wesley Church, with its exclusively European membership, remain exclusive? Or should the door of the church be open to all who wished to worship? African nurses from a hospital located a few blocks from the church had been dropping in for services, and some parishioners felt this should be encouraged. Others did not.

Finally, as reported to me, a woman who represented both town and farm—she lived in the country but worked in town—spoke. "We are a Christian congregation. We are part of a world fellowship of Christians of all races and nationalities. It is impossible for us to be exclusive and remain Christian. The Christian fellowship must always be inclusive. I move you, Mr. Chairman, that we go on record as remaining a Christian congregation, with the doors of the church open to any who wish to worship with us." The motion prevailed.

A truly Christian fellowship cannot be exclusive. It is inclusive or it is not Christian. Societies are divided in many ways—ethnically, professionally, economically, educationally, religiously—but truly Christian fellowship is indivisible.

America's current struggle for an inclusive fellowship is known and evaluated all over the world. From the African viewpoint, and probably from that of all non-Caucasians, nothing has done more to undermine the prestige of America and to cause people to question the relevance of churches than the discriminatory racial practices that still exist in our culture. The events of our civil rights struggle have been played up in newspapers, magazines, over the radio, and on television.

The Northern News of Zambia, on January 30, 1965, printed a picture of three husky white policemen bending over a Negro woman, the policeman in the center with his baton raised threateningly. The caption under the picture read: "Dallas County Sheriff Jim Clark uses his baton on a Negro woman as she bites and fights back after being thrown to the ground. Clark, centre, and two deputies were trying to handcuff the woman, who Clark said, had struck him in the eye. *She was in line trying to register to vote.*" (Author's italics.)

In its "Viewpoint" column of August 16, 1965, the *Times of Zambia* said, "The world stands appalled at the torrent of hatred now being released in America." The same issue carried bold-face headlines of rioting in Watts, "NEGROES STILL LIVE IN POVERTY," and the story went on to say, "Discrimination in employment, housing, and education, alleged police brutality and lack of community leadership were blamed today for Negro unrest which has flared into violence in this prosperous city."

Young missionary Judith Dodge (no relation) described the difficulty Americans overseas have in interpreting what is happening in their homeland; in 1965 she wrote from Japan, "Today I received a welcome letter from America giving the writer's observations on the racial situation there. You cannot know how carefully the actions of Americans are being watched here in Japan. . . . These Japanese interested in Christianity ask searchingly why racial problems exist in a 'Christian' nation."

The American image has been damaged badly, more by the underlying causes that make people feel their only redress is rioting and violence than by the riots themselves. Social restrictions and repressed frustrations of years—even generations—have caused the ever greater accumulations of emotional pressures to break forth in mighty outbursts of irresponsible demonstration and violence. The violence is against the segregated system, condoned and reinforced for decades by the churches that have permitted these injustices. As a result, the churches are being dismissed as irrelevant, in a time when relevance is of the utmost significance.

Perhaps the sharpest critics of the "Great Society"

are those from overseas who come to America on diplomatic missions or to study. In Africa and Asia they read about discrimination; in America they experience it. The bitterness of these experiences leaves deep wounds. Many present-day world diplomats studied here; the memories of their humiliating experiences do not enhance the American image, nor do they increase our bargaining power in a divided world.

One such contemporary leader was invited to speak at a missionary training conference during his student days in America. He arrived from the airport just as I was about to leave for church and accepted my invitation to accompany me. We went into a church and sat down. As we rose with the congregation to sing the first hymn, an usher invited my friend to leave the sanctuary and to sit in the empty balcony. We both walked out of the door of the church as the congregation sang on. Forecasts are that this young man, leader of a strong nationalist party that is striving for its country's independence, may well become the president of his nation some day. What will his attitude be toward the church? Toward America, where this episode was only one in a long series of discriminatory experiences?

Graduate student Daniel Kasambira remembers vividly the time he was invited to be a guest speaker on Missions Sunday at a Sunday school whose church supports a missionary in Africa. After he finished speaking, he was taken home—before the

church service began. The next Sunday he returned
to the same church to worship but was turned away
at the door. "These bigots do not bother me so
much," Kasambira wrote in January of 1966. "They
take a stand. What bothers me is *the thundering
silence of the nice people.*"

Most of the older generation are perfectly content
with the *status quo.* We make our necessary adjust-
ments to life in our youth or when we get married,
and from there on it is largely a matter of walking
in familiar paths. We feel at home in the familiar
social, psychological, and physical environment; we
know how others of our community or our set react,
and they have a fairly good understanding of our
reactions to known stimuli. We become relaxed in
our environment; it belongs to us and we to it. We
are secure in the circle we have created and which
has created us.

Because we are satisfied in our environment, confrontation is something we do not anticipate; we
fail to see or feel the storm clouds approaching until
they have broken over us. Confrontation may demand a change in our pattern of life; it may require
a complete new set of reactions. It produces more
than a squeak in our well-greased vehicle; the dis-
cordant note it interjects into our personal sym-
phony disrupts the entire harmony of our lives. Few
of us stop to ask from what the disturbance stems.
Why is it here? Where will it lead? We simply react
against it.

If we stop to think, confrontation can be a beautiful and hopeful sign that change is taking place and that we too can grow with the new that is coming into our lives. Change is a sign of life. On the other hand, it may be as unwelcome as a frosty morning that reminds us winter is near. A bit of confrontation may well be the eternal spirit prodding the crocus through the crusty earth. It may be as tender as the first awakening of love. It may be positive and creative. We need not react to civil rights confrontation as something evil. If we look at it positively and constructively, we will welcome it as from God.

Often we associate the word "violence" with physical force used by those who oppose us. Physical force, or the threat of it, is what we resent; we will *not* be coerced.

But there is another kind of violence—the violence that whites have practiced against Afro-Americans for decades and centuries. We Caucasians, as a group, have used *spiritual* violence, not physical, to manipulate people and events to our liking. We have not raised a hand against Negroes, but our attitudes have inflicted deep wounds on those we may have thought insensitive to such feelings (if we thought at all). We have assumed our superiority, their inferiority. It is we white people who have sat as judges. We have assumed our right to be served, theirs to serve; we have assumed our knowledge, their ignorance. The tone of our voices kept them in their places, but the lifting of an eyebrow can pierce just as deeply into a soul as can a steel sword the heart.

With physical violence we can prepare for the shock as we see it coming; afterwards we can estimate the damage done; we can feel some justification in retaliating. But spiritual violence is more destructive than physical, and often the damage done is unsuspected until physical violence descends upon *us*, in retaliation. In many respects, it is amazing that the accumulation of long years of spiritual wounds has not resulted in greater bitterness in the civil rights movement.

For the Christian, the damage done by riots in Watts, Newark, Detroit, and elsewhere must be considered less significant than that still being done by discriminatory social practices. Because physical damage can be estimated in millions of dollars we shudder to think of what each summer may bring forth in America. We react against physical destruction. We call for more law enforcement to protect our property. After recent summers we are a shocked nation.

It is not that I encourage or condone physical violence, but I think I can understand what causes it in the context of civil rights. It is, in part, the reaction against decades of spiritual violence. It has burst forth in excessive force because emotions have been repressed so long, and the hurt has been so great that something had to give. Negro violence may be considered the evidence that hope has been restored. The reaction is like that of the energetic boy, repressed in school or at home, who becomes a terror once he is freed from oppressive restrictions. It is similar to that of the adolescent lad who first confronts the authority of his surprised dad with a resounding "Go to hell!" It is similar to the reaction of a starving man who finds food: he overeats until his whole system revolts and he loses it all. It is the tendency to overdo once restrictions are slackened. It is the social pendulum swinging wide before it finds its proper arc.

No one who comes from an inferior position can be fully free until he has challenged those who have dominated him. The Afro-American cannot slide quietly into American society as a full adult citizen until he has proved to himself as well as to others that he has the strength to maintain his new-found status. The rise of Black Power is, in a sense, a concerted attempt to achieve recognition through confrontation of a society controlled by White Power. If the white blacklash retaliates, as some individuals are suggesting, permanent estrangement between two segments of the same society may result.

If the rise of Black Power and the riots in northern cities can be seen in perspective and dealt with wisely, if massive corrective measures can be taken promptly to remove the tinder which causes conflagration, the Negro may move quickly from junior to full membership in American society. But this will not happen unless the White Power block that considers itself the guardian of the American social structure relaxes sufficiently to welcome the Negro on a basis of equality. Here is a clearly defined task awaiting implementation by the church.

Let us not take too much comfort from the good civil rights legislation that has been enacted during the past few years; the struggle for an integrated society is just beginning. Legislation is important —laws must be on the side of justice—but the legal framework is impotent unless it is supplemented by the good will of the people.

An integrated society cannot be legislated. A process of reconditioning must go right into all of the fibers of our social, religious, and personal life; we must discipline ourselves to think charitably and considerately of others. We must go further than just determining to do good; we must effect a complete change of heart.

Because of my long sojourn in Africa and my identification with the African people, I have become suspect in the minds of some. I shall never forget my first encounter with a white churchman of some stature. He was talking with others of his rank when I arrived and was brought to be introduced. A spontaneous flicker of his eyes, an almost imperceptible shudder, an involuntary action of withdrawal belied the forced smile and extended hand he finally offered. I often encountered the same reaction when I met Roman Catholic priests in Angola, in the old days, but reactions there have changed to such an extent that I am encouraged to believe that a relaxed, conciliatory, and understanding relationship can be established between the races in America.

The most important single step in establishing this relationship in our materialistic society, after the spiritual one, is economic security. Because of our idolatry of the material, the current struggle focuses in the areas of employment, housing, and education—all of which bring material benefits. If victory can be achieved in these areas it will probably follow in others. But to appeal for fair play from prejudiced people is like throwing straws against the wind, for the function of prejudice is to defend interests, be they social, economic, political, or psychological.

The effectiveness of the civil rights movement— one of the most creative and dynamic social forces of the mid-sixties—has come from its shock to the ordinary, apathetic, self-centered citizen. It has forced the average white man to consider dialogue with the Negro on a basis of equality. The Negro has to be taken into account now; he can no longer be ignored. His presence is felt because civil rights demonstrations have made it known that the Negro, too, is an active part of American society; he is no longer a passive bystander. His decision during the Montgomery bus strike exploded something within the Negro himself: it announced to society that his years of passive subjection were over and that the "good old days" were gone forever. This announcement has made any curtailment of the forward march of civil rights a surrender. If the Negro does not continue his march to equality and fellowship and all that that involves, his children and their grandchildren will curse him for cowardice. There comes a time when a people must act or bequeath a bitter heritage to both history and posterity. The time for the Negro is *now!*

What is so unusual about any American who has the determination to get for himself and his descendents those things that the American culture considers of value? To the Negroes, white Americans have postulated spiritual qualities which they themselves do not possess. We have expected the Negro to be meek, patient, long-suffering, and obedient. We have expected him to turn the other cheek to both economic and psychological insults. We have expected him to practice the more refined spiritual graces that we only talk about. But the Negro cannot help but see what we consider the *real* values underlying white society. He also is an American.

What do the Negroes in America value and want? While there may not be unanimity among them, there is common assent to the major goal: *to belong,* to be acknowledged and accepted as mature members of society—local, national, or world. This acceptance includes the enjoyment of all rights guaranteed by the constitution and commonly enjoyed by most Americans. These rights are relatively simple: the right to live where one chooses, to engage in constructive and creative employment in keeping with one's abilities, to attend schools on a competitive basis, to have complete freedom of worship, to have the power of bargaining, and, of course, to vote.

In an adult education class for church workers in Cincinnati, in October of 1966, Samuel R. Wright, a local Methodist pastor, described these wants more graphically than I can ever hope to: ". . . to be treated as persons, not property; to be accounted men, not pawns; to be included, not forgotten; to be respected, not rebuked; to be treated justly, not as jokes."

We can easily accept these goals as reasonable and desirable for South Africans or Utopians; their realization will not affect our established way of life one whit. But to move over and share *our* comfortable seat with someone who has always stood? The change in the pattern of things is the rub. The demands—and they have become demands—are really not so unreasonable; we just had not realized that we might have to change *our* way of life, nor were we forewarned that we must change so soon. It takes time to adjust to change, but remember: change is not only in the air, it is fast becoming the order of the day.

Probably no institution at any time in history has been more "on the spot" than the Christian churches of the United States today. The key to the solution of the racial problem is in their hands; their members belong to every strata of society. All they need do is act decisively and concertedly to start a new wave of hope and optimism throughout our land.

But what is the record of the churches in the past? Can we look forward to an inclusive fellowship and an integrated society if they continue as they have? Most of us are well aware of the unsavory record:

The churches participated in the capture of slaves in Africa, even to baptizing them as they embarked down rickety gangplanks into the smelly holds of crowded ships. We compromised and removed Negro preachers from integrated colonial churches and permitted the establishment of separate houses of worship, where a doctrine of racial inferiority was preached.

Were only historical misdeeds to be charged against us we might still move forward to conquer the land of doubt and build an inclusive fellowship without agony. But the truth of the matter is we don't *want* to, even today. We still want to maintain the pattern of an exclusive religious fellowship that begat the child of social segregation. The churches have lived with this child for so long that we have forgotten that it is not the child of divine love.

Pagan Christians pay lip service to a gospel that proclaims a message of individual worth, but they deny a place within their fellowship to individuals redeemed by divine love—but not bearing their skin pigmentation. They hear the gospel but do not understand it; they may give intellectual assent, but that does not carry over into the emotions that control their conduct. They have fought against any change in the social pattern that would give Negroes the rights promised to them in the gospel.

When an integrated society comes—and come it will—it may be a dead victory for the churches. How can we rejoice emotionally or give shouts of victory when we finally accept, grudgingly, a fellowship almost forced upon us by legislation? Any victory celebration will bypass us. The churches may still have varied activities, stately buildings, and modern methods of communication, but something—something important, something vital—will have died by default.

Is there still time to avoid so calamitous an outcome for the churches? We have failed, it is true; but failure is a part of human frailty. Even so, not all have failed. There have been those, both black and white, who have been gloriously true to the heavenly vision. Some have paid the price of martydrom; others, ostracism; still others have suffered economically, physically, and emotionally for their stand on an inclusive fellowship.

An all-inclusive fellowship is not yet a reality, but an increasing number of clergymen and many laymen—especially women—are leading the crusade. There will be a new day.

V ❧•*A Materialistic Philosophy*

"In God we trust" appears on our coins, but the average American seems to put more trust in the coin itself. The newcomer to America, or the returning citizen, struggling to get to his hotel in the heart of New York City from a pier or airport, quickly realizes this hard fact as he copes with outstretched palms.

One fresh-minted diplomat from one of the newly independent African countries, after paying innumerable porters to transfer his luggage from customs to bus, to terminal, to taxi, to hotel, and from the lobby to his room, remarked, "If this is civilization, take me back to Africa!"

Even our rating of ourselves seems to be based on price tags more than on anything else, and "failure" happens only to the economically insecure. Swedish Bengt Simonsson, who attended graduate schools in Evanston, Boston, Syracuse, and Dallas, wrote, "Money and prestige, power and possessions are the indicative gauges of success." African Daniel Kasambira, studying at Ann Arbor, expressed much the same thought in more academic terms: "I wonder whether materialism has not become the way of life. . . . It appears very much like a student who majors in minors."

Another African student found high among American values the desire to "have things, to keep up with the Joneses, or a little ahead of them: modern kitchen, three bathroom house, wall-to-wall carpeting, motor boat, two cars, etc., so that instead of being at home with their children or there when they come home, the mother is out working. Children come home, no parent; husband comes home, no wife; or the wife is tired and crabby and there is no good, homecooked meal and certainly not a happy one."

Possession is not only "nine tenths of the law," it is part and parcel of the American culture. In the minds of most Americans the acquisition and accumulation of money is considered an evidence of virtue. A man's worth is judged in terms of the money he possesses or controls. Success in America is based on material accumulations. Failure is ascribed to those who struggle to keep their heads above water economically.

Several years ago a pastor friend of mine discussed possessions with a church-school class of youth. "How many radios do you have in your house?" he asked. One youngster came up with fourteen! Two, three, even four television sets per family were not unusual; indeed, the greater the number, the more they seemed to feel a part of the "Great Society."

Our social strata have also been determined

largely by our financial status—our right to belong to a club, to live in a particular community, to attend a particular school or university. At certain times, however, and in certain places, material values lose their meanings. Has our overdependence on material things made many Americans scrutinize this philosophy? Are some finding it wanting?

Certainly the decision made by two scions of well-known families—the Rockefellers and Roosevelts—to serve in VISTA was much publicized. Is the younger generation making the pendulum swing toward involvement, with the emphasis upon social values rather than materialistic ones? VISTA (Volunteers in Service to America), Operation Crossroads Africa, NTC (National Teachers' Corps), CUSO (Canadian University Service Overseas), and the well-known American Peace Corps continue to attract youngsters from all income levels, in addition to a large number of older people.

If this be true, what of the churches? Like most other social institutions, they too have climbed on the bandwagon of conformity and national materialism. In any struggle between God and Mammon, the latter has had an easy victory. Too many church people have forgotten Paul's admonition: Do not adapt to the pattern of the present world, but expect a transformation. By choosing to *con*form, they have surrendered their power to be *trans*-formed, for conformation and transformation are usually antithetical.

As in the rest of society, success in the ministry

of the church is usually gauged in terms of salary. An appointment is determined by the salary a church will pay. Progress from the circuit to the cathedral is well-regulated in not-too-wide financial steps. Generally speaking, a minister's salary makes it possible for him to associate on a basis of near equality with the social strata of the community he serves—a level determined by income. Any church vestry group knows that they must offer an increase in salary, or some other material attractions, in order to get the *right* man. My fellow ministers are enmeshed in a culture that stresses materialistic values.

There must be profits in business; otherwise the whole industrial and commercial enterprise of the world would collapse. Even idealists must live, but for the church to accept a philosophy of economic determinism simply means her demise as a Christian institution.

The church cannot compete with big business. If the idealism of sacrifice and service is lost she will have to accept only the "failures" of a materialistic society into her professional ranks. Let the church abandon the service ideal, and those with initiative and ability will naturally move into the more lucrative business world. Thus leadership in the church and in social agencies will be downgraded.

Then, too, the church will have lost both her platform and her voice, from and with which to judge the world. No one can objectively and effectively evaluate a system of which he is a willing and enthusiastic participant. Were the profit motive to be adopted openly by the church, the moral fiber of the nation would further deteriorate. There is still sufficient idealism within the church to challenge a philosophy of materialistic determinism and thus to hold it partially in check.

In all of life there needs to be a set of checks and balances. These checks disappear as the church accepts one after another of the standards set by a pagan world until she loses both her inclination and her power to evaluate and oppose. This has happened already to a dangerous degree in the matter of materialism. Remove from the church the idealism of service and sacrifice and substitute a purely economic motivation, and the already eroded standards will collapse and disappear. The Christian businessman—and there are still many of them—will gradually lose his incentive to serve, if the church which gives him spiritual nourishment abandons its idealism in this regard.

The boards of missions related to the National Council of Churches can question the New York banking consortium about its loans to South Africa only because they themselves have maintained certain ideals of justice and of service to mankind.

The rising importance of the laity in the local church is good. The laymen need to take more responsibility in their own churches, but they also face a great temptation—to apply to the church the methods and procedures of their business organizations. This increased involvement can be good if the profit motive is sublimated to human values. But materialistic values are so much a part of the thinking of the average businessman that he may think in the same vein when he works on church boards and commissions.

Many sensitive ministers face strong spiritual conflict. Some resign from the ministry because they feel that since the value systems of church and business are often the same they can either make a more vital witness as laymen or at least get full economic benefit from their labor. Some are troubled, as am I, with the fact that they are controlled by a value system that is alien to the gospel they are trying to proclaim. Many begin their ministry feeling that they were divinely called to serve. When they become aware of another value system within the structure of the churches, they may struggle against the unfairness of a fellowship that proclaims itself interested primarily in personal values but which, in fact, is largely materialistic in its values. They become the angry young men within the establishment. Others settle down to get the most the system has to offer, disillusioned and despiritualized.

Many, of course, are so much a part of their culture they have no conflicts. They become perfect props of the "American way of life"—by not understanding or by refraining from reading those portions of Scriptures that might disturb their own equilibrium or that of their congregations. They proclaim the glorious kingdom of comfort and economic security. Most pulpit committees do not expect their ministers to make the congregation uncomfortable, nor are they supposed to upset the children of their parishes with ideas of unrealistic idealism.

Pressures to conform to the standards of the community are great, and any minister who hopes to be considered successful will have to struggle with his own soul before he surrenders to the dictates of the vestry. Unfortunately, his supervising clergy may not be much help; they, too, may have been caught in the grip of the prevailing culture. Economically and ecclesiastically, the supervisors are nearing the top of the ladder of "success," and their policy is simple and understandable: economic progression follows ecclesiastic promotion. In our present structures there is little room for spiritual evaluation; much is measured in material terms.

The churches follow the pattern of the world in still another area. Their participation in the financial world is fantastic; they have multimillions of dollars invested, on which they depend for security. The churches have followed the cultural trends, and now, like the ministers, they are almost hopelessly enmeshed in the binding tentacles of materialism.

I like to meditate and attend services in worshipful sanctuaries as well as the next man, but I shudder at the paganism of spending millions of dollars on statues, stones, and plush carpets while millions of *people* suffer. Most of the great cathedrals of

Europe were built before and immediately following the Reformation and are monuments to the pride of bishops and monarchs. Here and there one finds a dynamic pulpit today, but most of them are relics —monuments to the past that are beautiful, magnificent, and awe-inspiring, but cold and irrelevant to the needy and hungry who walk and beg below their spires.

Several years ago, I spent an enjoyable half hour looking at the treasures of a historical cathedral situated between Rome and Naples. As I walked back to reboard my bus, the pleasure I had felt from gazing at the gold and precious stones—guarded under lock and key, and collected over many generations—dissipated rapidly. Of what use was the wealth of the *things* the cathedral possessed, when the poor and the hungry of that parish still walked hopelessly in the cold, damp streets around it?

As I travel through the States I find that many church people are apologetic when they show me their lovely and costly sanctuaries, their fully equipped educational units (many of which are used only once a week), their lavish social facilities. The guides on my tours have often tentatively suggested that perhaps too much has been spent for comfort for *that* congregation, while others are in need.

One of the most terrible aspects of our pagan, materialistic philosophy is what possessions do to *us*, the people who acquire them. Jesus' concern was always for people. Christian teaching will always confront materialism. Instead of using his needy neighbor to increase his material substance, the Christian will use his own time and energy as well as his material substance to help any who are in need.

Many large corporations make sizable contributions to charity, and for this we can only be grateful. The inquisitive might ask, however, where does the money come from? From the Latin-American peons who work on our plantations for less than a hundred dollars a year? From the black child labor of the Angola coffee plantations? From Mozambique miners who travel hundreds of miles and live in barracks away from their families for eighteen months at a time to mine the gold of South Africa?

Materialism uses people for gain; Christianity uses gain for people. The two are incompatible.

How can the churches bear any effective witness in the face of deadening materialism unless their leaders are free from its grasp? In the light of the needs of the world one must question the justification of high salaries in church-related administrative jobs. It would seem that there might be a minimum and maximum salary which would give freedom of operation for church executives but, at the same time, might make it possible to esteem them for spiritual qualities which the world also might begin to recognize. It should be *costly* to be a bishop.

A spiritually oriented leadership in the church should not need materialistic undergirding for its

authority and security. Only a spiritual ministry
can speak out against the evils in society. And certainly prophetic voices are needed in America
today!

Some residue of Christian idealism is still found
in the boards of missions of the various churches.
As idealistic young people volunteer for service
overseas, they are extracted from the prevailing
American materialism and given stipends in keeping with their actual needs. Many receive only a
half, a third, or a tenth of what they would receive
were they following their professions in the States.
The freedom from the materialistic values does
something for them spiritually, which may also
cause them to become misfits in American material-
istically oriented society. Often they return shocked
at the values they find in their homeland.

Probably the most disheartening attitude an overseas worker can encounter upon his return to his
homeland is the suggestion that he made a mistake
in freeing himself from the grip of materialism. Of
course it is not worded that way. A remark is
usually made about the sacrifices of missionary
work—how the missionary has surely done his
share and about the openings up the ladder in his
profession in the States. The assumption is that of
course he will want to make his peace again with
our glorious materialistic culture.

One gentle missionary doctor and his wife wrote
simply but meaningfully when they returned to the
States for their first furlough, "We both shiver at

the mass tendency toward waste." There it is. When
they lived in the United States they had not noticed
it, but coming back to the States after five years in a
culture where tin cans are carefully kept as drink-
ing vessels to a culture where discarded automo-
biles of recent vintage mar the landscape requires
adjustment and reconditioning—if one hopes to
live with his conscience in America.

This story brings into focus the whole question of
the immorality of our national extravagance. Not
only do we spend hundreds of millions of dollars
upon cigarrettes and alcohol which are actually in-
jurious to our bodies, but we gorge ourselves with
rich foods we neither want nor need. We overcon-
sume or discard *daily* almost enough to supply the
minimum requirements for a hundred million people. High-pressure advertisements induce us to buy
things we do not need and which we often regret
buying. At Christmas and birthday times we are
puzzled over what to give our loved ones because
they already have more white elephants on their
hands than they can house. The answer is to buy
more spacious and costly houses to store the things
we don't want. It's a vicious circle, getting bigger,
deeper and deeper, all the time. And while we
waste, there are those who lose hope, as much because of our lack of concern as because of their own
lack of physical energy.

The churches, which have been largely absorbed
into the prevailing pagan, materialistic culture pattern in America, have tried to maintain a different

standard for their missionaries and sister churches overseas. If they stop to think about it, this presents two sets of values within the same organization: one for the board members and executive staff living in America, another for colleagues serving overseas. Were the boards of missions to lead in the matter of salary equalization for staff and missionaries based on the cost of living, both overseas and in America, they might spark a new wave of spiritual idealism. It might do something for the fellowship to know that a missionary doctor in the Congo receives the same salary as a missionary bookkeeper, and that in America various administrative officers receive salaries according to the cost of living in their society, not according to the elevation of their office.

A friend of mine asks, "But what happens in a society where 'life' is defined in terms of money? Can the social 'givens' be changed?"

Before I attempt to answer that question, I want to add a few queries of my own. Is the church here to change the social "givens" to those in keeping with the gospel? Or is it here to accept the prevailing social values as the norm for its own life? Is the church here to exist harmoniously within the present cultural pattern? Or is it here to transform culture through the transformed lives of believers? Always we come back to the question: Is the Christian to *conform to the world* or be *transformed by* the image of Christ? The answer is clear. If the church would be Christian, it defines the abundant life in terms of relationships rather than in terms of material possessions.

The churches will never be dynamic spiritual forces unless they break with the pagan influences that have crept into the center of the household of faith, the most pagan and widespread of all being adherence to materialistic values.

"It is easy to criticize," says another friend, "but more difficult to make constructive suggestions. What do *you* suggest?"

A bold announcement that the churches repudiate the materialistic "givens" is my answer. If the churches established a *maximum salary* well below business standards—say, $12,000 a year—those who now receive more than that would have the satisfaction of knowing that their surplus was going to undergird the minimum sustenances of younger men or toward programs of evangelization and benevolence. If this were done, the churches might regain some spiritual power; prophetic utterances might again come from prominent pulpits of the land.

Although such a move might mean that some ministers and church leaders would move over into the business world, wouldn't such a move be helpful to both churches and business? Wouldn't it help upgrade the ethical practices of business and at the same time help the churches become the dynamic force they should be?

This problem is not a new one. Human characteristics have not changed very much in the course of

the years. One of the founders of American Methodism, Bishop Francis Asbury, wrote in 1801, "I cannot record great things upon religion in this quarter; but cotton sells high. I fear there is more gold
than grace, more silver than of 'that vision that
cometh from above.' " [1] The cotton continued to sell
well, for ten years later the bishop observed, "How
hardly shall preachers who are well provided for
maintain the spirit of religion!" [2]

Yea, how hardly do materialistic possessions and
spirituality keep intimate company! Camels still do
not pass easily through the eyes of needles.

[1] L. C. Rudolph, *Francis Asbury*, Abingdon Press, Nashville,
Tenn., 1966, p. 181.
[2] *Ibid.*, p. 107.

VI ❧•*A Compartmentalized Life*

When I was a boy growing up in a predominantly Protestant community, we used to think the Catholics were more fortunate than we. They could go to Mass for an hour on Sunday morning, considering that sufficient religion to last them for the whole week, whereas we had to be quiet and worshipful the whole Sunday through. But from Monday morning until Saturday night we were on a par with them. We had done our duty by our religion.

Of course, we were both wrong. We thought of religion as a set of observances to be periodically performed. Indeed, this concept of religion is childish, but many adults still cling to such ideas.

To a large extent, Christianity in America is still considered a carefully guarded compartment of life rather than a quality of life. As a compartment we believe it can be closed or opened at will; as a quality it colors and tones every thought of the mind, every spoken word, every tensing of the muscles, every emotion of the heart, every act. Any man's religion permeates every phase of his life, and it *shows* whether he wishes it or not. Thus, all who know him can tell if a man's god is money, possessions, prestige, comfort, pleasure, sport, or popularity, or whether he is a follower of Jesus Christ.

The tendency of the Westerner to try to separate his life into compartments is incomprehensible to the African. Within traditional Animism, religion was the thread which was interwoven through every phase of the social fabric. All phases of life were religious. The idea of the oneness and wholeness of life was never questioned. A man's religion could be understood in the things he did or refrained from doing. Is it any wonder the African cannot understand our attempt to set the secular apart from the sacred?

After spending several years in Africa and absorbing something of her values, I was taken aback by what seemed a double standard of friendship practiced in America. On Sunday morning our pattern of life calls for recognition in the form of a handshake or a friendly nod, but a similar encounter on the Wednesday commuter train may not bring forth even the flicker of an eyelid. Friendly greetings are for religious encounters, but in the business world eyes should be set straight toward the goal of gain, or at least on the empty seat of the crowded coach!

I attended a church meeting in the States at which the war in Vietnam was discussed. One church leader said feelingly, "Let us ministers keep out of the military field. I resent it when military men move into the field of religion." How compartmentalized can we get? Could there be anything more glorious than to have military men giving Christian witness through their vocal expressions and determined actions? What else was Jesus talking about when he instructed his followers to be witnesses in Jerusalem, Judea, Samaria, and unto the uttermost parts of the world? On all occasions, in every place, people should bear witness to their faith. As a matter of fact, they do so, whether they realize it or not.

Military men have a right to say something about the proclamation of the gospel. Ministers of the gospel and priests could also say something relevant about a nation's involvement in war. The Old Testament refers to the beating of swords into ploughshares and spears into pruning hooks; the New Testament speaks of being motivated by love. How can we be gratified by the oft-released statistics of Viet Cong killed in battle, yet claim to comprehend the gospel of love as an abiding and conditioning force in our lives?

I don't believe in violence of any kind; neither do I condemn the young men of this and past generations who dutifully, sometimes unwillingly, have defended and still defend the interests of their nation in armed conflict. But ministers of religion (indeed *all* Christians) do have the right—even the duty—to rise up and speak out about the pagan methods of settling disputes still being used in this "enlightened" era. They may not have the right—nor should they attempt—to direct military operations, but Christianity definitely has something to say about the totality of life and death. Until churchmen clarify, in their own minds, the incompatibility of war with the gospel message of love, we can have little hope of eliminating any kind of mass violence, be it in Vietnam, Detroit, or the Congo.

A friend told me of an experience he had in a World War II canteen. A group of soldiers burst in to celebrate their safe return from a hazardous bombing mission over Germany. One of the young airmen carried a cup of coffee over to my friend's table and sat down.

"I was brought up to think coffee-drinking was a sin," the youngster remarked as he drank with obvious relish. "I hope the Lord will forgive me."

It didn't seem to occur to the young man that the destruction of German lives might call for prayers for forgiveness! What have we been teaching in the name of religion?

We ministers and religious leaders must be held at least partially responsible for presenting the fragmented scriptural teaching that results in such blind spots—a teaching that becomes a contradiction or an evasion of the total gospel truth. In this light, think of the moral conflicts and emotional pressures chaplains must go through. They prove their heroism and devotion when they leave families and comfortable parsonages to serve the youth of this and other nations. At the same time, their position must be most difficult as they try to harmonize the gospel of love with the destruction and inhumanity they witness. On the one hand there is the loss of lives on the enemy side; on the other, the tragic distortion of values and the physical and psychological suffering of their charges.

In *The Comfortable Pew* Pierre Berton reports that a survey revealed that on questions of morality in modern warfare chaplains differ little from other service officers. More than half deny that any conflict exists between military regulations and religious ideology; 79 per cent believe that a man with a good religious training will make a better soldier; 45 per cent go along with the view that killing any enemy soldier is a righteous act, and the remainder think it justifiable; none feel that the individual soldier has any moral responsibility in the matter except to serve his country.[1] Isn't this attitude evidence of the impotence of modern churches? Or is the support given to a destructive national war machine only an indication that even eminent church leaders still fail to view life or the gospel in its totality?

For many years the minister considered himself responsible only for man's soul—meeting the spiritual needs of his parishioners. The doctor took care of man's body; the teacher, the mind. Today both medicine and theology repudiate this compartmentalization.

Medical schools and seminaries alike realize that if man—body, mind, and soul—is to be ministered

[1] Pierre Berton, *The Comfortable Pew*, J. B. Lippincott Co., Philadelphia & New York, 1965, p. 67.

to effectively, he must be approached in his totality. Many modern hospitals use teams of doctors, social workers, and ministers, who work together to meet the total needs of their patients.

Some churches also call in psychiatrists to work with ministers and doctors of medicine. Each helps the other to see the interrelatedness of different phases of personality and the inseparableness of the physical, psychic, and spiritual. In *Minister and Doctor Meet,* Granger E. Westberg points out:

> Religion, after all, is concerned with man's attitude toward all of life, not with some little segment of it which some people would label the 'religious.' When a person accepts the Christian way then it ought to color every aspect of his life, including the physical. . . . The Christian faith sees man's spiritual problems always in the context of his day-to-day existence in a real world with a body to feed, a job to perform, and someone to care for.[2]

Many people, however, have not effected this transfer in their own thinking. For them, separation of church and state means that religion must limit itself strictly to the church; the state, to politics. Times and places for religion to function include church worship, baptisms, weddings, and funerals; the remainder of life is given over to secular activities. Such compartmentalization suggests that man lives in a two-story house—the secular occupying the ground (and most used) floor and the

[2] Granger E. Westberg, *Minister and Doctor Meet,* Harper & Row, New York, 1961, p. 53.

sacred occupying the second, with no connecting stairway between the two. We talk of the sacred temple in the secular city as though one were holy, the other vulgar, and divide our personalities as we attend to our duties in each.

Both the secular and the sacred intermingle in life and flow through our very same veins. An experience of giving of self in a sex experience in the home can be holy; a service in a church can be obscene although it goes under the name of worship. It is not the place, the time, or the element that makes one thing holy and another profane. Holiness comes from obedience to the Spirit of God and sin is an act of disobedience. Holiness is something we can do with our whole self; sin is that which does not have the consent of our unified personality and consequently sets the various members warring among themselves.

Worship can become sinful and divisive when the whole personality doesn't enter into it. Pretense in the churches makes those who use it divided personalities. The true self is obscured for the sake of personal or family reputation. Thus worship, which should unify man as it brings him into the presence of the divine, becomes a lighthearted game of role-playing instead.

The ineffectiveness of a faith restricted to Sunday school may be responsible for the loss of personal morals. What does being a Christian mean to young people in our churches? What about the unwed mothers who bear 300,000 babies each year in America? The millions of others—both men and women—who engage in promiscuous sexual intercourse? What does a compartmentalized religion have to say to the playboy who goes to church with his established family on Sunday and shares the apartment of a single-girl companion on Tuesday and Thursday evenings? How many of the world's twenty million alcoholics are Christian in name and upbringing? How many of those arrested for crimes of violence once received communion or religious instructions in our churches? What of the mentally ill who occupy half of our hospital beds? What does the breakdown in the social fabric of America say about the ineffectiveness of a compartmentalized faith limited to the Sunday school?

Several years ago I happened to be in Johannesburg, South Africa, at the close of the revival and healing campaign of a well-known revivalist. His campaign was a "spiritual" success, but the leader was stopped by secret police at the Jan Smuts Airport for attempting to leave the country without declaring a valuable diamond. How hard it is for ethics and piety to meet in a compartmentalized religion!

Too often our children realize that what we profess is not our real belief. Anthropologists tell us that the self man deliberately tries to project may not be the real self and that we cannot transfer what we do not possess. If we have no positive faith, how can we hope to transmit anything but spiritual bankruptcy to our offspring?

We cannot transmit a positive faith simply by employing new church gadgets invented by modern industry. No matter how costly the set or attractive the television promoter may be, or how soothing the radio voice of the announcer, or how intense his hot-line promotion, any attempted transmittal will be a failure if the salesman does not believe sufficiently in his faith to live it himself.

Religious faith is transmitted by example. It reaches into every phase of human experience and activity just as oxygen in the blood aids in the renewal of all living cells. A pretense of faith cannot do that any more than a veneer can change the real grain of wood or a rinse permanently remove the gray from our hair. Modern gadgets can be useful, but they do not change the quality of life; that must come from the center outward. And come it will, be it positive or negative.

Most of us do not realize how plainly our children, our neighbors, our friends—even our pets—read us. We are an open book. This was demonstrated to me in an unusual way not long ago, but I need to take the reader back a few years to begin my story:

After Dag Hammarskjöld died in an airplane accident in what was then Northern Rhodesia, the Swedish people wanted to build a lasting memorial to their fellow countryman who had served the world so well as Secretary General of the United Nations. They decided to build a library on the campus of the Mindolo Ecumenical Foundation, near the copper-belt town of Kitwe. After the beautiful building was ready, books began to arrive, but there was no trained librarian available; so the Board of Governors of Mindolo asked the Swedish people for another favor—a trained person to catalogue the books and to train Africans to do the work in the library. The Swedish people sent Miss Marianne Asplund, an experienced librarian from Stockholm, for a two-year period.

When she first arrived on campus Miss Asplund was lonely and felt foreign. A stray cat came to her notice, and she adopted it. It made her little duplex apartment more like home to come back to at the end of her work day. She treated her cat well, and it was very contented. Miss Asplund, too, came to feel very much at home in Africa and settled into her work with satisfaction.

As she neared the end of her two-year stay, Miss Asplund felt conflicting emotions. Although she was glad to go home, she was sorry to leave sunny Africa and the many friends she had made there. She tried to see beauty spots she had not had time to see before. She had to arrange for her trip back to Sweden. She had to pack. All of these activities upset her usual routine and made her rather nervous and tense. And her cat became apprehensive. She began following Miss Asplund to the library or to the neighbors' doors—wherever Miss Asplund went the cat was sure to go.

One day Miss Asplund entered the campus chapel

after the first hymn had been sung. She shut the door quietly and took a back seat. Suddenly the morning meditation was shattered by a series of loud meows. Then the cat appeared at an open window on the platform and leaped softly inside. She sniffed the feet of the worshipers until she found her mistress and there she curled up at Miss Asplund's feet. While the students and staff turned their attention back to the morning speaker, I mused on that cat. Why had it become so insecure, after two years of contentment? What made it so fearful of losing its good friend? Miss Asplund might have talked to her cat, for all I know, but surely it could not have understood that Miss Asplund was going away. Still, it had read the signs— the nervousness, the tenseness, the upset daily schedule. And it responded with nervousness, too. If a cat can sense emotions in a human being, how much more can our human associates do so! They know when we are filled with frustrations. They do not need to be told when we have serene faith. We communicate the totality of what we *are*.

Churches and churchmen must realize that the only way to transmit religious values is to incorporate them into the fabric of our lives. When Christian faith is real it becomes ingrained in all of life, and we have no trouble transferring the positive values of our faith. When that happens within our churches, we can expect a revival of dynamic religion to reach out across the land.

In no area of society is the gap between Christian *practice* and *ethics* more pronounced than in that of race relations. From the very beginning of our national life the churches considered it expedient to save the soul of the Negro rather than to liberate his whole self. In his biography of Bishop Francis Asbury, L. G. Rudolph points out that economic pressures, in the early 1800's as now, often dictated policy: "Finally he began to yield. If there had to be a decision between working at anti-slavery agitation and working at evangelization of the South, it was clear where his choice lay. Evangelization must come first. Increasingly, then, he shifted from attempts to emancipate the Negroes." Later, Rudolph added, "The economic drive for slavery was plain. . . . The price of slaves kept rising." [3]

We may excuse such a clear-cut and fairly deliberate attempt to separate the spiritual from the physical and psychic—to save the soul and let the body break in serfdom and the mind stagnate in ignorance—two hundred years ago, but what of the present-day continuation of this practice?

From South Africa I have just received a letter from an outstanding Caucasian preacher, a man of great evangelizing zeal. Said he, "It is better to win one soul for Christ than to integrate a thousand who continue on their way to a lost eternity." In spite of having been brought up in Africa, this evangelist still separates man's soul from the totality of his being. He gets great comfort from "saving souls"

[3] Rudolph, *op. cit.*, p. 181.

but is uninterested in programs of social better-
ment, justice, and freedom.

Some Christians in America also continue to divide man into different compartments so that gospel passages about love and justice do not interfere
with goodly profits. Personal piety is good; devotion
to the church is pleasing; evangelizing zeal is com-
mendable—*if* all are exercised within the framework of the gospel and its emphasis on the wholeness of man.

Jesus exemplified that quality of wholeness
wherein the fragments of life are brought together
into a fully integrated self. This wholeness gave
him much of his authority and power. Our churches
have lost much of *their* authority and power because of their fragmented approach to life—a split
organization or institution is as impotent as a split
personality. While we have developed a pseudo-
Christian society that still retains many Christian
values, pagan or non-Christian forces have introduced extraneous values and practices into the totality of life.

It is impossible to confine religion to the church
or to a single compartment of life. We delude
ourselves if we think that only the practices we
perform in church represent our true religious expressions. Often these are simply socially accepted
veneers that cover temporarily the true grain of our
lives.

This discrepancy between what we *are* and what
we try to represent ourselves to be causes many

observers to discredit the effectiveness of the gospel within our cultural pattern. African Daniel Kasambira expressed this thought when he wrote:

> I also see that church members have so diluted Christianity that they have come to feel that true religion is what transpires on Sunday morning in a building with gothic architecture. To them the laity is a well-dressed group of auditors who sit comfortably in their pews observing and listening to a performance by the clergyman and choir. Therefore, they think that what goes on through the week in factories, schools, homes, shops, and offices has no bearing on their Christian lives and commitment. They also act as if religion belongs to the professionals—missionaries, clergymen, and full-time lay Christian workers. In short, the laity are spectators rather than participants.

Our task is to make the gospel relevant to all of life. An editorial writer described this task bluntly in the *Times of Zambia* on Christmas Day of 1965: "The trouble is that religion is pretty much in retreat. Clergymen keep talking about 'putting Christ back into Christmas.' They won't do it, unless they can discover some way of putting him back into the other fifty-one weeks of the year." [4]

[4] *Times of Zambia*, "Viewpoint," December 25, 1965.

VII ❧∙∙*A Living Hope*

An institution I know has lovely tall white pillars in front of one of the public buildings, a library dedicated to the memory of a benevolent and gracious bishop of The Methodist Church. Unfortunately, pigeons have discovered that the tops of the pillars under the overhanging roof make an ideal roosting place. In the evening they come from far and near and spend the night on the tops of the pillars. The messy results can be imagined. At any rate, the pigeons have kept the students from leaning against and lounging around those pillars. The wary students using the library at night have learned to walk circumspectly between them.

The problem of the pigeons might be solved in one of five ways: destroy the pigeons, change their habits, endure the unsightly mess they cause, shoo them to some other roosting place, or tear down the pillars. The second possibility is probably the least likely to succeed; pigeons have pretty fixed habits and they are not likely to reform.

Fortunately, what applies to pigeons does not apply to man. Man can reform or, better still, *be transformed.* The culprits need not be destroyed or even shooed to some other church. Neither need we wallow in the mire of our sins or tear down the ineffective building. Man *can* be redeemed, and through a transformed humanity our churchly problems can be solved.

"I told you so; he belongs to the establishment!" many will say. If advocating redemption aligns me with the establishment I am glad to be so identified, for what other hope is there for the problems that cry out for solution?

I have not enjoyed pointing to some of the tragic aspects of the American church life, but speaking out has afforded me a certain sense of relief. Many of the criticisms I have made throughout this book I have wanted to say within the councils of the church, but neither the opportune time nor the appropriate place ever seemed to present itself. My opinions have been suppressed for many years; some may have mellowed with time; others may have become more highly tempered. Some white columns of stately structures may have been unfairly scraped; some stiff white shirts or clerical collars erroneously ruffled; but I hope that there are enough small kernels of truth in the bulk of the chaff to prove that a problem *does* exist.

Four attitudes can be adopted in our less-than-ideal church situation:

Force legislation and compel compliance: Legislation is essential, but we must not be overoptimistic, for no amount of legislation can make us one or unite our divided community and fragmented witness. Oneness is something that emanates from the heart; it cannot be imposed from without. Legislation can make us conscious of the need for unity, but it cannot, of itself, bring about unity. Unity can be realized only if everyone sees the other fellow as a well-loved brother; if we ignore denominational tags and national identifications; if we look at the personality of the individual, not his color. Legislation cannot compel anyone to accept another as a brother beloved; only redemptive love can—and does. Those who advocate legislation must realize that even the most just and benevolent laws cannot create automatic unity; it must come as a quality of life.

Conform to the existing culture: These problems have always been with us; why worry? If Christianity, in nearly two thousand years, has failed to produce a Christian culture, will it ever do so? The mainstream of the pagan-Christian culture probably is not going to change. Why not get with it? Let's climb on the bandwagon of the "Great Society"; proclaim the "American Way of Life"; take what they have to offer and don't be too concerned if the American reality impinges on the Christian ideal. We must give lip service to the ideal, but lip service shouldn't get us into too much trouble—at least not often.

Ideals are good, even necessary for children, but the present structure seems to be pretty well anchored—indeed, hard as a brick wall and rigid as a steel beam! It may be as cold and unresponsive as a cake of ice at times, but that's life. Polish the apple, squeeze as you polish, then sit back and enjoy the drops of juice while they are fresh and sweet.

Let the reformer advocate change or become a missionary, let the legalist legislate and the angry young men from the lower strata of society use violence, let the idealist chant; as for me and mine, we'll remain respectable and enjoy life all the way up the ladder. Possibly, because we haven't disturbed the *status quo,* we'll get a three months' vacation and a world tour as our reward. Then, after getting some additional comprehension of the world situation, we might become moderator of our synod at the next biennial assembly.

Reform—by force, if necessary: Let the structures rock and topple, cry the angry young men; the creative spirit within Christianity will make new ones more in keeping with Jesus' teaching and the needs of our day. If, because of its rigidity, the old cannot be remodeled to suit the spirit of the hour or meet the current needs, the sooner it is toppled the better.

Must injustices continue just because they have been worked into an antiquated structure? Must we always wait for a full consensus before we speak on issues that demanded our voice last month? Must we be guaranteed a soft landing place before we jump? Or must we be sure that we have an electric blanket before we retire for the night?

I must admit that I have a certain understanding for this frame of mind and a certain sympathy for the viewpoint. Youth always cries out, "How long, oh, how long must we endure the archaic and antiquated, the rigid forms, and the dry bones?" I say, my heart goes out to them in their impatient desire to see the Kingdom come. They are the Peters who reach out a sword to slice off the ear of him who would shackle Jesus. To those youth—and to those not so young—who are willing to endure hardship and to see old structures topple and take their chances on rebuilding new ones more modern and more functional, I would offer a word of caution: *The structure may not be so important as the people who fill it.* To a certain extent the structures do make or break the man, but it is also true that the men and women in it determine the quality of the structure. Generally speaking, a vote against the church structures is a vote of no confidence in the men who fill those structures.

No matter what the form of structures of the churches, there are certain administrative functions to be performed. These may vary from denomination to denomination; but I have seen nonepiscopal leaders become more authoritarian than many bishops I know. I have also seen pastors and even laymen in the local church dictate more than episcopal leaders would think of doing. It is the people who make and maintain desirable or undesirable structures. Therefore the solution to structural problems is not in the structures themselves but in the quality of people placed and maintained in them. Again we come back, as we always must, to the quality of life of the individual.

Commit our existing problems to a concerned Father: And then do everything *we* possibly can to work toward a practical solution. Most problems in life are spiritual and require a spiritual solution. Still, we can't expect God to do the whole thing for us. As St. Paul said, "We are workers together with God."

Transformation of the human heart comes from contact and association with the Divine nature, or any portion of it, by association with God through Jesus Christ.

Our part in trying to achieve a purer and more worthy church as well as a less pagan society is threefold. First, *we must seek a spiritual solution for ourselves.* Essentially this means that we must surrender our wills to the divine will. As Jesus prayed in the garden, "Not my will but thine be done," so we also must come to the place of surrender to the Higher Power. With that surrender will come a pardoning of offenses and a cleansing from sin. Then we become ready for the daily walk in obedience to the dictates of God's will.

The Holy Spirit regulates our relationship both to God and our fellow men. He removes colored glasses from our eyes and masks from our faces. He leads us into new truth. His presence within us generates filial love, which reaches up to God, and brotherly self-giving love, which goes out to our fellow men wherever they may be found.

Without the surrender of self, any kind of spiritual solution is most unlikely. We are dependent upon God for his acts of mercy, love, and grace, but our part is not passive. We must respond to his generous love and forgiveness by accepting new understanding and truth as he puts it before us.

Second, *we must also confront our brethren with the meaning of the gospel,* as shown to us, even though they be more mature and more powerful than we. God may entrust some of his less authoritative sons with spiritual insights hidden from churchmen under pressure of constant meetings and travels. "Out of the mouths of babes" comes much sense, as so many parents have learned! Confrontation must be developed more fully so it can permit some of the more modest to become Balaam's asses, through whom God may speak to his imperceptive prophets.

Third, *like-minded Christians must work together,* across all kinds of lines, to achieve, as far as is humanly possible, the realization of their dreams for a meaningful church in a society awakened to the need for brotherhood. Leaven from within can infuse new spiritual life into the entire churchly lump. An inclusive fellowship is both a challenge and an inspiration. As has happened within the state church in Europe, fellowship groups can bring about considerable change in the spiritual climate. In due course they may be able to influence greatly the structure of the church.

My hopes for the spiritual renewal of the churches are based on (1) faith in God, (2) faith in people, and (3) faith in the constructive outcome of current restlessness.

(1) *Faith in God:* God has never left the world without a faithful witness. If effective witness cannot be made within the established churches, He will raise up a witness elsewhere for our day. Perhaps it will come from the so-called "fringe groups."

From Norway to Portugal, from Mexico to Argentina, it is the Pentecostal groups that are making more than a vocal impact on the social structures of the nations. In many respects I do not agree with them in their narrow, pietistic approach to life and religion; but that matters not a whit if they are being used of God to proclaim an eternal message being neglected by the established churches. Their loyalty to Christ and their dedication to a cause make their witness the most effective of our time in many areas of the world, even though they also have their blind spots. The message must be proclaimed by the best means at God's disposal, even if it is limited and partial. It would seem that he does not require a perfect channel through which to work (how fortunate for us frail human beings!). But he does require dedication to himself.

How glorious it would be if God could use for

renewal the churches he has used so mightily in the past! How he must long for both dedication and enlightenment! If he cannot find that combination, the witness—fragmented and incomplete—will still be made. Whether God will use my church, or any other "established" church, will depend upon whether we seek to do his whole will in all of our lives. The defects in the churches are ours, not his. My hope for renewal comes from my faith in the Great Creator, the Great Renewer, whom we call God.

(2) *Faith in people:* I have considerable confidence in people, both individually and in groups. A Scottish friend of mine remarked once that he liked Americans singly but found them hard to take collectively. I think I can understand what he meant. When I meet Americans singly, they are more themselves. Yet I have faith in the fairness of both the individual and the group—especially a group that claims an allegiance to Jesus Christ and his principles. Sometimes the latter takes a bit of prodding to keep it awake to the issues at hand, but it does have a foundation of basic beliefs and goals.

There are individual churchmen, lay and ministerial, who are outstanding in their devotion to the church. Others are dedicated to their particular denomination. Sometimes I get disturbed when I hear loyalty proclaimed to John Wesley as if he had been substituted for the Holy Spirit in the third place in the Trinity, or at least were vying for authority with the Pope! While these leaders of the churches may be children of their culture in time and geography, most of them are more than representatives of a temporal, regional denominationalism; they are men and women searching for the imprint of Christ. Some come closer to finding it than others, but all of them have certain qualifications and abilities, of which spiritual insight is not the least.

"God's road is all up hill, but do not tire. Rejoice that we may still keep climbing higher," said Arthur Guiterman. After we pass the sixty-year mark, our natural tendency is to settle down at the foot of Mt. Horeb. But the vision of a promised land and a faraway glimpse of an unfulfilled dream can be tantalizing. The ideal is still there, but the human dynamics to realize it have been partially dissipated in maintaining the establishment. The will to move forward, however, is not altogether lacking, even if the senior saints have to be carried. This will to move forward is part of our living hope.

Pope John's creative leadership inspired not only Roman Catholics but all Christians. Seldom in human history has a man of his age undertaken to initiate such a movement of renewal. If God can raise up such a man for our time of urgent need, how can we give up hope that the spirit of renewal will continue to operate throughout Christendom?

(3) *Faith in the younger element of church life:* The younger generation is definitely on the move. Sometimes that movement appears to be only in circles, but as I ride the missionary circuit I meet with many groups of restless young ministers—and

some not so young—within denominational lines and outside any single denomination. Most sensitive church administrators are aware of the restlessness and may wish, as do I, that the movement had more direction to it. This feeling of restlessness also exists among missionaries. Will the old structures withstand the beating at the door, the shaking of the foundation? If the restlessness be only of man, they probably will—but if it be of God?

Are We Yet Alive?—a provocative booklet by Pauline Webb, a sensitive and wise churchwoman from overseas—describes this tide of renewal:

> In some places it is still only a distant rumble, a rumor of things astir, but in others it has already come flooding in, sweeping away so many of the structures of church life that once seemed permanent, but now appear to have been built only on the sands of time. If we in Methodism are to be caught up in this great flood-tide of new life, then we too shall have to be prepared to see many of our traditional strongholds fall as we hear the call to launch out into the deep ocean of God's love for the world.[1]

If the restlessness that grips our dissenters in this great land of material abundance is the same kind of Christian idealistic restlessness of which Miss Webb writes, we should give God thanks for each attempt at reform or renewal. Those at the heart of existing structures should study carefully the unusual clouds appearing on the horizon, lest their

[1] Pauline M. Webb, *Are We Yet Alive?* Epworth Press, London, 1966, p. 9.

strength and purpose be underestimated or misunderstood because of the youthfulness of those seeding them. Thirty seems to be a dangerous age, an age of both idealism and action, as history has amply recorded. These dynamic qualities are part of our living hope.

How are we going to make that hope a living reality in a truly Christian church? Perhaps we do not need to go beyond the churches in our present thinking, for once the churches become truly Christian they will then be what Paul suggests as the Body of Christ—*the* Church—and it will make its impact upon society.

"But," the question is often asked, "wouldn't it be better to think only about the individual's relationship to God?"

"No!" We have done that far too long. We must *begin* with the individual and follow him as he moves into the Christian fellowship in Christ, which is *the* Church. But we must not leave him alone or he will stagnate. There is also the community, the state, the world of which he is a part. He must make his witness in all of these widening circles of relationships and create in them a sustaining fellowship.

"Yes!" We *begin* with the individual, with ourselves as we first meet the newborn babe in Bethlehem's manger. We sense the humble setting, the unconcern of the animals as they chew their cuds of hay, satisfied when their bellies are full; they are only animals. We observe the tenderness of a mother's love as she cares for her infant son; we reflect on the mystery of birth, the potential of life, the uncertainty following death. These things play upon our emotions and bring forth a deeper response than that of the casual traveler or curiosity seeker. Slowly the thought comes to us that this babe is also ours; he belongs to the world. We bow in adoration.

At the other end of the spectrum is a tired figure trudging the incline of Golgotha between two soldiers. Three crosses are erected, and to the center one he is nailed. Blood flows. It is a nasty, earthy scene, followed by a hurried burial; but it is also followed on the third day by his glorious reappearance. Then, just before the ascension, he gives his last solemn testimony and a commission to his followers to witness to these things among all people to the ends of the earth. *We* have been commissioned.

Some of the events are beyond our experience and therefore of our comprehension; some are unclear. We may have difficulty formulating our doctrine. But the call to worship is clear. Following the act of dedication will come the direction. Robert Spike, in *The Freedom Revolution and the Churches*, rightly states, "There must be a deed before there can be a doctrine that makes sense. Commitment is not a decision to do something about belief, it is the belief that comes from having acted obediently to Christ, with self-concern pushed to one side." [2] Our living hope is the nature and depth of our commitment.

We must place human values before material ones, look at our material resources in the light of human need everywhere, and view human need everywhere in the light of our material resources. *In The American Class Structure*, Joseph Kahl writes, "At the very top are the one per cent of family units who have an income of over $15,000. . . . They live in 'great luxury' for they are plutocrats. . . . At the bottom of the scale are the twenty per cent of family units that receive less than $2,000 a year." [3] That is the American scene. The contrast in the world scene is even greater. Unquestionably what we have to do with and what we do with it says a great deal about the depth of our commitment. How can we challenge a materialistic society if we become a bedfellow? Or eat at its well-furbished table? Can we in the upper economic brackets effectively witness to those in middle or lower brackets, if our sharing is only verbal? Jesus saw this problem clearly: "Ye cannot serve God and Mammon." If we compromise in this practical test of our discipleship, we shall compromise in others. Christ and his church await our choice.

A full commitment to Jesus Christ means becoming part of an inclusive fellowship. All denomina-

---

[2] Spike, *op. cit.*, p. 83.
[3] Joseph A. Kahl, *The American Class Structure*, Holt, Rinehart & Winston, New York, 1957, p. 120.

tions, all classes, all nationalities, all races have their rightful place in a Christian fellowship—on a basis of equality. All belong in the Christian church if their lives are linked to God through Christ. We must decide to do what Lerone Bennett, Jr., bids us do in *The Negro Mood:* "What is required now is an act of the spirit. We must abandon our shallow trenches and confront each other as co-inheritors of a common land, which is to say that we must meet and know each other as brothers in a marriage of vision, as co-conspirators in the making of a dream, as fellow passengers on a journey into the unknown." [4]

A full commitment to Jesus Christ leaves us no option, for as we become one in him we become brothers to all. Our brotherhood cannot be superficial; it must be what we know in Africa as blood brothers, but in this instance it is the blood of Christ the Savior that unites us. Is there a plainer way to say it? Is there a way to make this more emphatic? Certainly contradictions in the gospel do not divide us. Our shallow commitment causes our tragic divisions.

Our commitment must be to a Person—not to a structure, an organization, or an establishment. We may commit ourselves to these as well, but we must always keep foremost our main commitment. As an insect sheds its shell, one structure may give way to another; structures may bend and sway in the

[4] Lerone Bennett, Jr., *The Negro Mood,* Ballantine Books, New York, 1964, p. 101.

winds of time, but fellowship must remain clear, distinct, and inclusive.

Commitment to Jesus Christ means involvement from where we are to the ends of the earth. His Kingdom knows no geographical boundaries. Wherever he is found we must be also, or we shall break the ties that join us to him and to each other. Our space age makes it easier each day to follow him all over the world, preparing lives for the building of nations, helping us to involve ourselves in the spreading of the gospel.

Commitment means the giving of self in life and death. It extends from the cross to the grave; it includes public and private life, pleasure hours as well as professional. It is as operative at sunset as at sunrise, in good times and bad, at home and over the world. Commitment is an allegiance originally given to Jesus Christ and daily renewed. The initial act of self-giving may have been done through an emotional struggle, or it may have come about gradually and smoothly. Whatever its beginning, it must be repeated until it becomes a quality of life. If the perpetual obedience to the will of God should bring us, like our leader, to a cross, we know that in the cross there is radiant hope.

Thank God we are not pigeons—we are men. Through God's grace we can be transformed. Here is our living hope.